VISUAL GRAMMAR

Picture it!

Practise it!

with answers

Jim Scrivener

 Richmond

Richmond

58 St Aldates
Oxford
OX1 1ST
United Kingdom

© 2013, Santillana Educación, S.L. / Richmond

Publisher: Deborah Tricker
Digital publisher: Luke Baxter
Content development: Anna Gunn
Editors: Eileen Flannigan, Stephanie Parker
Design and layout: Lorna Heaslip
Cover design: Mark Willey
Photo research: Magdalena Mayo
Art direction: Helen Reilly, Lorna Heaslip

With Key Edition ISBN: 978-84-668-1529-1
CP: 502599
D.L. M-8267-2013

Printed in China

Publisher acknowledgements:
*The Publisher would like to thank all those who have given
their kind permission to reproduce material for this book:*

Illustrations:
David Broadbent, Phill Burrows, Karen Cheung,
Ella Cohen, Pete Ellis, James Gilleard, Ben Hasler,
Dave Oakley, Ben Swift, Eva Thimgren

Photographs:
J. Jaime; J. Lucas; ALAMY; CORDON PRESS/Corbis;
GETTY IMAGES SALES SPAIN/Photos.com Plus, Thinkstock;
HIGHRES PRESS STOCK/AbleStock.com; ISTOCKPHOTO/
Getty Images Sales Spain; PHOTOGRAHERS DIRECT;
REX FEATURES / SIPA ICONO; SEIS X SEIS; SUPERSTOCK;
ARCHIVO SANTILLANA

*Every effort has been made to trace the holders of copyright
before publication. The Publisher will be pleased to rectify
any errors or omissions at the earliest opportunity.*

Contents

Contents

Contents

Contents

Hello! My name's Jim and I'm a language teacher. My students find grammar difficult … and *I* find grammar difficult when I'm learning other languages. So, I wanted to write a grammar book that could help you understand grammar better and make your study a little bit easier.

Learning English

If you want to learn English well, you need lots of **language**.

You need **words**.

cat   guitar   happiness   cooker   window   tree   traffic light   hope

You need **collocations** and **chunks** – patterns of words that often go together.

blonde hair   fast food   have a bath   a cup of coffee   pass an exam   give up

You need to know **common expressions** and **when to use them**.

Excuse me   What a pity!   I'm terribly sorry   Let's go!   Could you tell me the way to …

You need to know the **pronunciation** of all these things (not just on their own, but when they are spoken in sentences).

hill   heel   /fɪʃ ən tʃɪps/

And you need **grammar**.

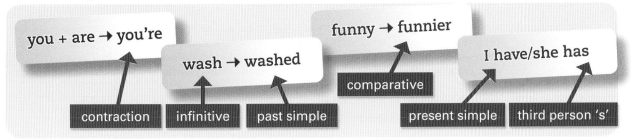

you + are → you're   wash → washed   funny → funnier   I have/she has

comparative

contraction   infinitive   past simple   present simple   third person 's'

It's not important to know grammar names like these. But it IS important to understand how the grammar works.

Of course as well as this, you need lots and lots of **practice**.

Practice … **Listening** to English. **Speaking** English. **Reading** it. **Writing** it. **USING** it!

To the student

Why do I need grammar?

You can communicate using just words without grammar – but your meaning will not be 100% clear.

Tony send Mary email.

It's like looking at a photograph that is out of focus or too dark. We have some idea of the meaning – but we aren't certain.

If we add grammar, we know much more, including:

time – when something happens

number – whether things are single or plural

actions – who does the action, how they do it and who they do it for or do it to

message – whether it's a statement, negative, question, request, order, etc.

Did Tony send Mary any emails?
Tony isn't going to send Mary that email.

Suddenly, our photo is clear and in focus.

This book will help you study grammar

Grammar is not just about studying the patterns, word order and endings. You need to understand the meanings and uses too. This book will help you with all of these.

English grammar is sometimes very strange. For example, a tense called the Present Simple can be used to talk about past and future times, not only the present! In some grammar books you will find all these different meanings in one unit, or even on just one page. This can be very confusing for students. So, in this book, I give a whole unit for each meaning. You will understand the language more clearly and will have much more practice in using it.

Grammar practice doesn't have to be boring!

Do the exercises like games. Do them again and again. Write them. Speak them. Record yourself saying them. Listen to them on the bus or tram. Try and remember them while you are walking in town. Write text messages to your friends and use the language. Test each other. Cover the page and test yourself. Look at the pictures – can you remember what was on the page?

Most of all, enjoy it. See if you can find why learning a language is exciting, interesting and fun.

Good luck!

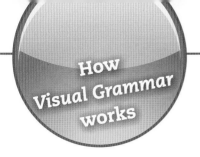

Grammar boxes

The grammar boxes show you how to make the grammar. You will find the 'rules' of the language and examples.

Pictures

The pictures help you understand the meaning of the language. They also help you remember the grammar.

Exercises

The exercises give you lots of chances to practise using the language. Sometimes different answers are possible.

About you

Some exercises ask questions about your life, your friends, your ideas, things you know etc.

The tough one

These questions are a little more difficult than the others. For example, you may need to think harder or use your dictionary to help you.

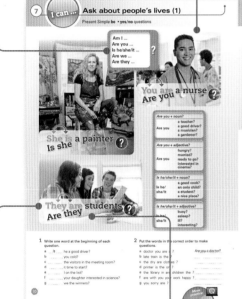

Examples

There are lots of example sentences. They show you how the language is used. The examples show real English – as people speak it – not just 'Grammar book' language.

Diagrams

The diagrams give you information about how the language works. For example, they show you that you must change the word order – or that you must change a word. Sometimes there are **timelines** that help you understand when something happens.

Internet quiz

In some exercises, you use the internet to find answers.

Word pool

Some exercises are word pools – a mixture of words. You must try to make sentences using the words. Many different answers are usually possible.

Present Simple **be** • **It's** + adjective

It + is = It's

It's long.

It's short.

It's old.

It's far away.

It's near.

It's tall.

It's beautiful.

It's huge.

It's big.

It's broken.

It's small.

---

1 Use the adjectives above to describe the pictures.

a

It's huge!

b

c

d

e

f

2 Write sentences about each thing.

a the Great Wall of China
It's long. It's old. It's beautiful.

b the Eiffel Tower

c the Mississippi

d the Taj Mahal

e the Sun

f the Great Pyramid of Khufu at Giza, Egypt

g my home

More practice

Present Simple **be** • **It's** + weather • **It's** + time

It + is = It's

It's cold. It's freezing.

It's windy.

It's sunny. It's hot.

It's cloudy.

It's stormy.

It's rainy. It's wet.

It's three o'clock.

It's a quarter to eleven.

It's midday.

It's five forty.

It's midnight.

It's ten past four.

It's a quarter past six.

It's half past nine.

It's ten to twelve.

1 Write the time in words.

a   *It's six o'clock.*

b   ....

c   ....

d   ....

e   ....

2 Complete the sentences with the words in the box.

> ~~freezing~~   half   It's   rainy   to

a Put on some warm clothes because it's ....*freezing*.... today.

b 'What's the time?' '...................... five o'clock.'

c We're late! It's a quarter .... nine!

d Take an umbrella. It's very .... outside today.

e It's .... past eleven. I must go to bed!

3 *ABOUT* YOU

Write about the weather in your country.

a In January, it's usually ....

b In June, it's usually ....

c In November, it's usually ....

Present Simple **be**

1 Match the sentence beginnings with the endings.

a Hello. Nice to meet you. I'm ...
b I live in Milan, but I'm ...
c It's my birthday today! I'm ...
d I left university last year. Now I'm ...
e Ha ha! No! Ted isn't my husband! I'm ...

1 25.
2 a sales manager.
3 Sue Cornish.
4 single.
5 Australian.

2 Complete the sentences with *'m, 're/are* or *'s*.

a Meet Marc. He 's a great designer.
b They _____ a really happy family.
c This is my wife, Jenny. She _____ a doctor.
d These young people _____ all college students.
e My name _____ Terry. I _____ an architect.
f Mrs McLeod _____ the new CEO of our company.

3 Complete the sentences.

a Harry isn't English. _He's_ Scottish.
b I don't know Maria. I think _____ Brazilian.
c Please be quiet, boys! _____ very noisy today!
d Mr and Mrs Jones work together. _____ both cooks.
e I'm the same age as my best friend. _____ both seventeen.

4 ABOUT YOU

Write five true sentences about yourself.

a (your name) _____
b (your job) _____
c (nationality) _____
d (married?) _____
e (age) _____

More practice

I'm ...

happy
hungry
worried
thirsty
cold
surprised
frightened
bored
tired

I'm
You're
He's
She's
It's
We're
They're

1 Say how **you** feel.

a

I'm hungry.

b

....

c

....

d

....

e

....

f

....

2 Complete the sentences with *am/'m, are/'re* or *is/'s.*

a She ....'s.... excited about the holiday.

b John .... worried about the exam.

c The children .... happy today.

d The weather .... really hot!

e Your hands .... very cold.

f Susie .... angry about the referee.

g The dog .... tired.

h The dogs .... tired.

i Luis .... frightened of spiders.

3 *ABOUT* YOU

Say how you usually feel at these times.

a before lunch
  I'm hungry.

b late at night, before bedtime

....

c before holidays

....

d before an exam

....

e before a party

....

Present Simple **be** + prepositions of place (**in, on, at**)

Oh no – my wallet's in the car.

Help! The cat's on the table. The food's on the floor!

My sister's photo is in the newspaper!

in ...	on ...	at ...
the car	the table	work / school
room 213	the shelf	home
the newspaper	the train	lunch
the cupboard	the first floor	the back
the bed	the agenda	the doctor's
		the crossroads

Your room is at the back of the hotel.

My parents are at work.

Our offices are on the ground floor.

on the bus

on the train

on the plane

in the car

1 Complete the sentences with *in*, *on* or *at*.

a The books are __on__ the shelf. The laptop's __in__ the cupboard.

b I'm not _____ work. I'm ill today. I'm _____ bed!

c The IT department is _____ the third floor. The warehouse is _____ the back of the building.

d We have a meeting today. Is it _____ room 6? What's _____ the agenda?

e Hi, Janice? I'm _____ lunch with Mr Abdul. My notes are _____ the office table. Could you bring them, please?

f Hello? Speak louder, please. I can't hear you... Yes, I'm _____ the train. I'll be home soon.

2 Where is my phone?

a

It's in the car.

b

_____ room 2B.

c

_____

d

_____

e

_____

f

_____

More practice

I can ... Say what is **not** true

Present Simple **be** • negatives

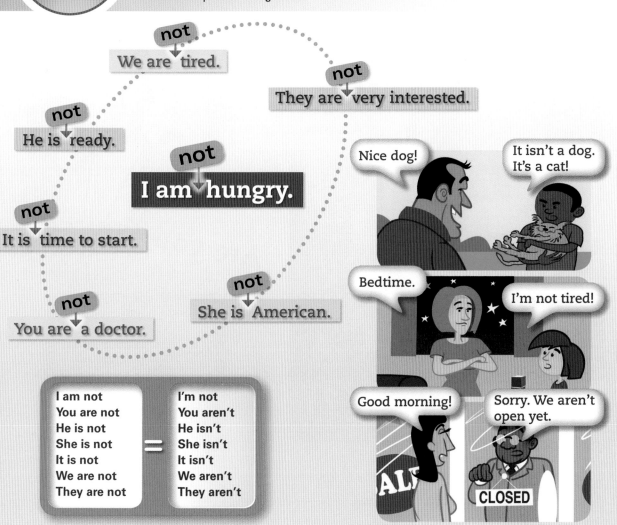

not
We are tired.

not
They are very interested.

not
He is ready.

not
I am hungry.

not
It is time to start.

not
You are a doctor.

not
She is American.

Nice dog!

It isn't a dog.
It's a cat!

Bedtime.

I'm not tired!

Good morning!

Sorry. We aren't open yet.

CLOSED

I am not	I'm not
You are not	You aren't
He is not	He isn't
She is not	She isn't
It is not	It isn't
We are not	We aren't
They are not	They aren't

1 Match sentences a–f with replies 1–6.

a Let's go.
b Pass me my diary, please.
c Could I speak to Melinda, please?
d What's the capital of Mongolia?
e I'm going to the Moon!
f Can Robert see the film with us?

1 No. Sorry. He isn't fifteen yet.
2 Sorry. She isn't in the office.
3 Don't be silly! You aren't an astronaut!
4 I'm not ready!
5 I can't see it. It isn't here!
6 Hmm. I'm not sure. Is it Ulaanbaatar?

2 Make the sentences negative.

a She's a good singer. _She isn't a good singer._
b This film is boring. ....
c I'm very hungry. ....
d We're late. ....
e Mark's a doctor. ....
f I'm surprised about it. ....
g Her story is true. ....
h It's very rainy today. ....
i They are from Sri Lanka. ....

3 ABOUT YOU

Add *is/isn't* or *are/aren't* to make true sentences about your hometown.

a My hometown .... famous.
b It .... very big.
c Visitors say that the shops .... interesting.
d The cafés and restaurants .... good.
e The weather .... usually very nice.
f Most people .... happy to live there.

Present Simple **be** • **yes/no** questions

Am I ...
Are you ...
Is he/she/it ...
Are we ...
Are they ...
?

You are a nurse
Are you a nurse **?**

She is a painter
Is she a painter **?**

Are you + noun?	
Are you	a teacher? a good driver? a musician? a gardener?

Are you + adjective?	
Are you	hungry? married? ready to go? interested in cinema?

Is he/she/it + noun?	
Is he/she/it	a good cook? an only child? a student? a nice place?

They are students
Are they students **?**

Is he/she/it + adjective?	
Is he/she/it	busy? asleep? ill? interesting?

1 Write one word at the beginning of each question.

a   __Is__   he a good driver?
b   .... you cold?
c   .... the visitors in the meeting room?
d   .... it time to start?
e   .... I on the list?
f   .... your daughter interested in science?
g   .... we the winners?

2 Put the words in the correct order to make questions.

a doctor you are a ?   *Are you a doctor?*
b late train is the ?
c the dry are clothes ?
d printer is the on ?
e the library in are children the ?
f are with you your work happy ?
g you sorry are ?

More practice

Give short answers

I can ...

Present simple **be** • short **yes/no** answers

Yes, I am.
Yes, you are.
Yes, he is.
Yes, she is.
Yes, it is.
Yes, we are
Yes, they are.

No, I'm not.
No, you aren't.
No, he isn't.
No, she isn't.
No, it isn't.
No, we aren't.
No, they aren't.

8

1 What answers does Tim give to Bruce?

Bruce	Tim
a That's my pen!	**1** Yes, they are.
b These chips are cold!	**2** Yes, she is.
c Peter's so funny.	**3** No, it isn't!
d Are we late?	**4** No, we aren't.
e Are you excited about the party?	**5** Yes, he is.
f Is she your new girlfriend?	**6** No, you aren't!
g I'm ready!	**7** Yes, I am.

2 INTERNET QUIZ

Answer the questions. Find pictures of the <u>underlined</u> words on the internet to help you.

a Is <u>Uluru</u> a very large rock? *Yes, it is.*
b Is <u>Rapunzel</u> a girl? ....
c Is <u>camembert</u> a drink? ....
d Are the <u>Monkees</u> a football team? ....
e Is the <u>Aintree Grand National</u> a car race? ......
f Is <u>penicillin</u> a drug? ....
g Is <u>Baloo</u> a tiger? ....
h Are <u>sweaters</u> clothes? ....
i Is <u>Ganon</u> a person in a computer game? ....
j Are <u>turacos</u> birds? ....

3 ABOUT YOU

Write true short answers. Use your dictionary to help.

a Is this book about grammar? *Yes, it is.*
b Are you good at Maths? ....
c Is it windy today? ....
d Are you a good tennis player? ....
e Is it after midday? ....
f Is your dad a good cook? ....
g Are you a football fan? ....
h Is your teacher in the room? ....
i Are your books in your bag? ....
j Is this a noisy room? ....
k Is the television on? ....
l Is your best friend funny? ....

4 THE TOUGH ONE

Write true short answers. Use your dictionary to help.

a Are you a nail-biter? *Yes, I am. / No, I'm not.*
b Are you a vegetarian? ....
c Are you left-handed? ....
d Are you allergic to penicillin? ....

More practice

17

Present Simple **be** • **Wh-** questions

When/Who/Why/How/What/Where + is/are + ... + ?

When + is	When's
Who + is	Who's
Why + is	= Why's
How + is	How's
What + is	What's
Where + is	When's

⚠ What + are → ~~What're~~ What are
Where + are → ~~Where're~~ Where are

What is the answer?

What are the answers?

When's your birthday?

Who's your tutor?

What's your name?

How's your sister?

Why's he late?

Where's your book?

How old are you?

1 Match the questions with the answers.

a Where are you from?
b How old are you?
c Where is your hotel?
d When's your birthday?
e Who's your best friend?
f Why are you in Great Britain?
g How good is your English?

1 Near the British Museum
2 July 9th
3 Sarah.
4 I'm at university.
5 I'm Hungarian. I'm from Budapest.
6 It's not bad!
7 I'm nearly 20.

2 Read the job interview. Complete the questions with the words in the box.

Are you   How old   What are   ~~What's~~
When's   Why are you   Why's

Kasia   Good morning.
Manager   Good morning. Let's start.
          _____What's_____ ª your name?
Kasia   Kasia Kazmierski.
Manager   _____ ᵇ are you, Kasia?
Kasia   I'm 22.
Manager   _____ ᶜ British?
Kasia   No. I come from Poland.
Manager   _____ ᵈ here in Britain?
Kasia   I'm finishing my university courses.
Manager   _____ ᵉ your graduation?
Kasia   In September.
Manager   _____ ᶠ your subjects?
Kasia   Hotel Management and Marketing.
Manager   _____ ᵍ our hotel interesting for you?
Kasia   Oh, I really like it. It's very old and beautiful.

3 Write a question word in each sentence. (Different answers may be possible.)

a _____Why_____ are you late?
b _____ are you from?
c _____ much are these postcards?
d _____ is the show?
e _____ old is your sister?
f _____ are the toys broken?
g _____ are the instructions?
h _____ are you today? Feeling better?

4 Use the word pool to write six questions.

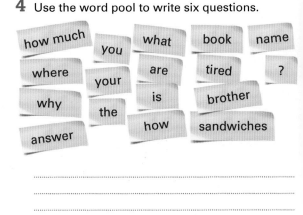

how much   you   what   book   name
where   your   are   tired   ?
why   the   is   brother
answer   how   sandwiches

....
....
....
....
....
....

More practice

There is ... / There are ...

Oh yes, Marie! Rio is fantastic! I love it! There's a beautiful mountain called Sugarloaf Mountain.

There aren't any clouds in the sky!

There are lots of beaches – like Copacabana.

There isn't any time to rest!

Look! There's a plane. There are two helicopters!

Are there planes in the airport? Yes, there are! There are 6 ... 7 ... 8 planes! Yes. 8 planes.

Is there an airport? Yes, there is! Wow! An airport in the sea!

There	is/'s	an airport.
	isn't	any rain.
	are	three helicopters.
	aren't	any clouds.

Questions

| Is | there | a nice beach | ? |
| Are | | good cafes | |

Short answers

| Yes, | there | is. | No, | there | isn't. |
| | | are. | | | aren't. |

1 Marco's friend says 'Tell me about Rome'. Complete Marco's sentences with *There's* or *There are*.

a *There are* a lot of lovely churches.

b .... a huge Roman theatre called the Colosseum.

c .... a lot of old Roman buildings.

d .... a river called the Tiber.

e .... seven famous hills in the old city.

f .... famous films about Rome – like *La Dolce Vita*.

2 Complete the questions with *Is there* or *Are there*.

a *Are there* advertisements on that website?

b .... a strange woman outside the building?

c .... eggs in the fridge?

d .... a shopping mall in the town centre?

e .... a printer in the office?

3 **INTERNET** QUIZ

Search for the underlined words. Use a dictionary or the internet to help you. Give short answers.

a Is there <u>nitrogen</u> in the <u>air</u>? *Yes, there is.*

b Is there real <u>gold</u> in the <u>Bank of England</u>? ....

c Are there <u>wallabies</u> in <u>New Zealand</u>? ....

d Are there wild <u>elephants</u> in <u>Malta</u>? ....

4 **THE** TOUGH **ONE**

Answer the questions.

a How many seconds are there in an ordinary year?
There ....

b How many dots are there in total on a pair of dice?
There ....

c Inuits live near the North Pole and are very good hunters. But why don't Inuits eat penguins?
There ....

More practice

I can ... Talk about friends and relations

Possessive adjectives

Sue's my mum. Brian's her husband.

This is Tom. I'm his sister.

Brian Sue **my parents**

my brother Tom

He's our teacher.

Mr Spark **my teacher**

I'm Daisy.

my best friend

Alice

1 Look at the pictures. Daisy is talking about people in her life. Complete the sentences.

a Brian is ___my___ dad.

b Sue is _____ wife.

c Tom's _____ brother. So, Brian and Sue are _____ parents and we are _____ children.

d We have a pet. Barney is _____ dog.

e I like Alice. She's _____ best friend and I'm _____ best friend.

f Alice and I are in Mr Spark's class. We are _____ students.

g We all love heavy metal! *Metallica* is _____ favourite band.

I	my
you	your
he	his
she →	her
it	its
we	our
they	their

Who is **your** best friend?

2 Complete the sentences with *my, your, his, her, our* or *their*. (Different answers may be possible.)

a Excuse me. Is this ___your___ pen? It was on the floor!

b This is the Palmas' house. And this is _____ garden.

c Why did she come back? Oh – she forgot _____ phone.

d Hello! Come in. Sorry – _____ home is very untidy!

e My boyfriend and I love *Alien*. It's _____ favourite film.

f Did you finish _____ homework?

g Mr Pipino is a banker and Mrs Pipino is a History teacher. _____ daughter is studying Biology at Buenos Aires University.

h Do you know _____ secret? He's a millionaire!

3 Choose two words from the box to complete each sentence. (Different answers may be possible.)

his their ~~your~~ her my its our
economy ~~house~~ lunch boyfriend
shoes favourite homework

a Let's meet tonight. Can you tell me where ___your___ ___house___ is?

b I can't come out now. I'm doing _____ Science _____ .

c Our country is having problems with _____ _____ .

d Tom's by the front door. He's cleaning _____ _____ .

e Irina says _____ _____ is very clever.

f Jodie and Izolda are in the kitchen, cooking _____ _____ .

g We like all the pictures in the exhibition, but this one is _____ _____ .

More practice

have got / have + noun

I've got a cat.

I've got a nice, small house.

I have two sisters.

I have a good job.

I've got a problem.

I have some good ideas.

I've got		I have
I've got		I have
You've got		You have
He's got		He has
She's got	=	She has
It's got		It has
We've got		We have
They've got		They have

UK

have got and *have* are both used.

USA

have is normally used.
(*have got* is less used.)

1 Which sentences are true about you?
Write ✓ (true) or ✗ (not true).

a   I have an old mobile phone. ....

b   My dad has a beard. ....

c   We have a cat at home. ....

d   I've got an older sister. ....

e   My house has got three floors. ....

f   I've got some money in my purse. ....

2 Write sentences with *has / have got*.

a

My parents *have got a red car.*

b
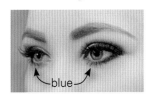
large
I ....

c

new
I ....

d

blue
Jane ....

e

The students ....

f

Juan ....

3 **ABOUT** YOU

Write a true sentence about each thing.

a   something in your pocket   *I've got seven coins in my pocket.*

b   something your friend has   ....

c   something your mum has   ....

d   something your family has   ....

e   something your teacher has   ....

f   something your school has   ....

More practice

have got / have + illness

Mike has an awful headache.

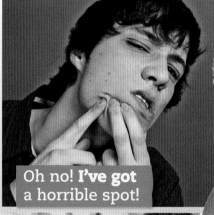

Oh no! **I've got** a horrible spot!

I've got / I have

a cough.
a fever.
flu.
a sore throat.
a high temperature.
a stomachache.
a toothache.
something in my eye.
a horrible spot.

She's got a cold.

I have a terrible backache.

1 Complete the sentences. Write **one** word in each space: *have, has, 've* or *'s*.

a Jack isn't at work today. He ____has____ flu.

b I ate some prawns! Now I _____ got a stomachache!

c 38 degrees! He _____ got a very high temperature.

d I can't see! I _____ something in my eye!

e Everyone is ill today. We _____ all got sore throats.

2 Which picture goes with each sentence in **1**?

3 Make new sentences for pictures that aren't in **1**.

4 THE **TOUGH** ONE

Complete the email from Amy Pepper's mother to her teacher. Say why Amy is not at school. Use your own ideas.

Dear Miss Clare,
I'm sorry Amy is not at school today. She _____ _____ . In fact, all the family is ill! Her brother Tommy _____ and I _____ . I hope Amy can come to school tomorrow.
Best wishes,
Angelina Pepper

More practice

Have you got and **Do you have** questions

Have you got your bag?

Have you got your phone?

Have you got your books?

Do you have any money?

Do you have a sweater?

Have you got the address?

Have you got my iPad?

Yes!

No!

Have you got		Do you have	
Has he got		Does he have	
Has she got	=	Does she have	?
Has it got		Does it have	
Have we got		Do we have	
Have they got		Do they have	

What have you got? = What do you have?

What have you got in that bag?	Clothes
What food do you have?	Two bananas
	Biscuits

1 Put the words in the correct order to make questions.

a sweets got any you have ?
  Have you got any sweets?

b correct she does the answer have ?
  ....

c you moment have a got ?
  ....

d have everything we got ?
  ....

e brown he eyes eyes does blue have or ?
  ....

f suggestion you have a do ?
  ....

2 Complete each question with **one** word from the box.

do   does   ~~got~~   has   have   you

a Have you ....*got*.... a cold?
b What do they .... in that box?
c .... this book got a good cake recipe?
d What answer .... you have?
e Where's my book? .... Min have it?
f Hello, Maria! Have .... got my purse?

3 Make questions for Isobel to ask John. Use the words in brackets.

John	I haven't got a bike.
Isobel	(car) *Have you got a car?* ᵃ
John	I don't have a grammar book.
Isobel	(dictionary) Do .... ᵇ
John	My aunt has got lots of pets.
Isobel	(dog) Has .... ᶜ
John	I don't have any cash.
Isobel	(credit card) Do .... ᵈ
John	I want to write the email address.
Isobel	(pen) Have .... ᵉ
John	Michelle's going to the concert.
Isobel	(ticket) Does .... ᶠ
John	Let's have a coffee!
Isobel	(time) Do .... ᵍ

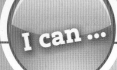

Short answers: **Yes, I have / No, I haven't / Yes, I do / No, I don't**

Aaargh! Hundreds of questions!

Oh no! More questions!

Have you got a pet? Yes, I have.

Do I have a car? Yes, I do.

Has your husband got a driving licence? Yes, he has.

Do I have a big family? No, I don't.

Has he got a passport? No, he hasn't.

Does my house have a garden? Yes, it does.

Have you got a child? No, I haven't!

Does my mother live in England? No, she doesn't.

Have you got a bike?	**Yes, I have.**
	No, I haven't.
Has she got a cat?	**Yes, she has.**
	No, she hasn't.
Do you have a fridge?	**Yes, I do.**
	No, I don't.
Does the house have a garage?	**Yes, it does.**
	No, it doesn't.

1 Complete the answers.

a Has Ahmed got a cold? *Yes, he has.*

b Does this school have a playground? Yes, ...

c Have you got a minute? Yes, ...

d Do you have sugar in your coffee? No, ...

e Do they have a house near here? Yes, ...

f Have we got today's newspaper? No, ...

g Does the building have a fire alarm? No, ...

h Has the farm got a certificate? Yes, ...

2 INTERNET QUIZ 🔍

Answer the questions with true, short answers.
Search for pictures of the underlined words.

a Does <u>Jupiter</u> have a big red spot? *Yes, it does.*

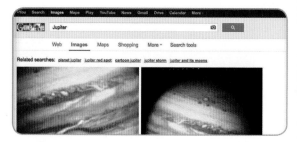

b Have you got a <u>ruler</u>? ....

c Have your parents got a <u>dishwasher</u>? ....

d Do you have a <u>screwdriver</u>? ....

e Does your school have a <u>hall</u>? ....

f Does your town centre have a <u>statue</u>? ....

g Have you got <u>posters</u> on your wall? ....

h Has your favourite swimming pool got a <u>roof</u>? ....

More practice

I can ... Talk about things I haven't got

Negatives: **haven't got** and **don't have**

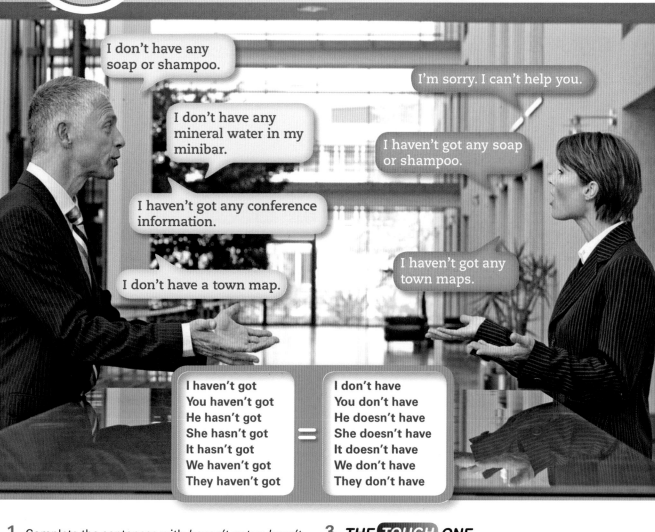

I haven't got	I don't have
I haven't got	I don't have
You haven't got	You don't have
He hasn't got	He doesn't have
She hasn't got	She doesn't have
It hasn't got	It doesn't have
We haven't got	We don't have
They haven't got	They don't have

1 Complete the sentences with *haven't got* or *hasn't got*.

a We __haven't got__ any rice so I'll cook pasta tonight.

b I _____ a lot of money. Let's buy something cheap.

c Don't ask him. He _____ any ideas.

d I _____ your book! Ask Sandra!

e Sarah says she can't drive you because she _____ a car.

f My parents _____ a computer. They use mine!

2 Complete the sentences.

a Emir hasn't __got__ his tram ticket.

b This is a great town, but it _____ have a cinema.

c We _____ got any eggs.

d Your dog _____ got a collar. Is it lost?

e The students _____ have an exam today.

f Her soup _____ got any salt in it.

3 THE TOUGH ONE

Match the expressions with the meanings. Check on the internet or in a dictionary if you don't know.

a I haven't got a clue.

b He hasn't got the message.

c I haven't got a penny.

d He hasn't got a hope.

1 No money!

2 No understanding!

3 No possibility of doing something!

4 No idea!

4 INTERNET QUIZ

Search for pictures of 'Manx cats'. Then complete the sentence.

a Most Manx cats haven't got _____ .

Search for 'planets and moons'. Then complete the sentence.

b Most planets have moons – but _____ and _____ haven't got any.

Search for pictures for 'bald'. Then complete the sentence.

c A bald person hasn't got any _____ .

More practice

25

this, that, these, those

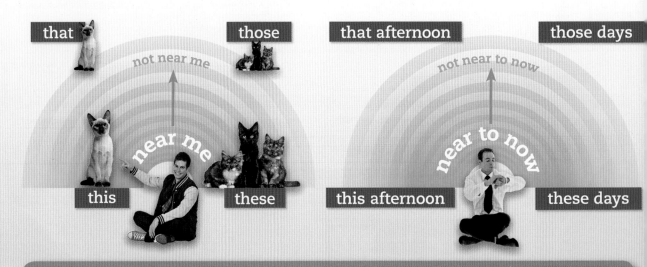

that	those	that afternoon	those days

not near me

near me

not near to now

near to now

this	these	this afternoon	these days

We can use *this* and *that* to:
- introduce people: 'This is Mike '
- start a phone call: 'Hi! This is Sue'
- check who is speaking to you on the phone: 'Is that Hans?'
- talk about what someone said: 'That's a good idea.' 'That's wrong!' 'That's great!' 'I didn't know that.'

1 This is Mike's room. Complete the sentences with *This is*, *That's*, *These are* or *Those are*.

a _____This is_____ my bed.
b .... my bike.
c .... my computer.
d .... my books.
e .... my phone.
f .... my pictures.
g .... my cat.
h .... my glasses.
i .... my guitar.
j .... my lamp.

2 Ivan is on a ship sailing down the River Thames in London. Use *this*, *that*, *these* or *those* to complete his sentences.

a _____This_____ ship is huge.
b Look! .... tall clock tower is 'Big Ben'.
c Oooh! .... wind is terrible!
d .... buildings are called 'the Houses of Parliament'.
e Look! In the sky! .... 's a Boeing 787!
f I want to move. .... chairs are very uncomfortable.

3 Sylvie is phoning Maia. Complete the sentences with *this* or *that*.

Sylvie	Hello? Is _that_ ᵃ Maia? ....ᵇ is Sylvie.
Maia	Yes! It's me. Hi Sylvie!
Sylvie	Zak just phoned me. He can't come to the concert with us.
Maia	Oh. I didn't know ....ᶜ . But Lena's coming, yes?
Sylvie	Yes. ....ᵈ's right.
Maia	Can I take my six-year-old?
Sylvie	Yes. ....ᵉ's fine. Look. I'll meet you at Reception at two o'clock ....ᶠ afternoon. OK?
Maia	.............ᵍ's great! Thanks.
Sylvie	.............ʰ's all right! No problem!

More practice

I can't play keyboards.

I can't act.

I can't answer that question.

I can't hear you!

I can't go to London next week.

CAN ✔ ➡

⬅ CAN'T ✘

I can play the guitar.

I can design a web page.

I can do this homework.

I can sing.

I can see you!

can / can't

If you *can* do something
• it is possible to do it
• you know how to do it.

I/You/ He/She/It/ We/They	can can't	run a half-marathon. speak Spanish. drive you to the shops. help. book the hotel for Tim.

can't = cannot

In speech we usually say *can't*.
We say *cannot* when we want to make it stronger.

Questions

Can	I/you/ he/she/it/ we/they	pay? sign here, please? find it? come round now? believe it?

Short answers

Yes, No,	I/you/she/he/it/we/they	can. can't.

3 Use the word pool to write six sentences.

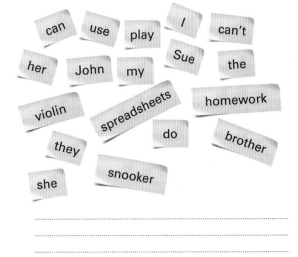

can use play I can't

her John my Sue the

violin spreadsheets homework

they do brother

she snooker

....
....
....
....
....
....
....

1 Tick (✓) the things you can do.

a cook Thai food ....
b ride a motorbike ....
c use Photoshop ....
d play squash ....
e read Spanish ....
f say *yacht* ....
g play the piano ....
h tweet ....
i repair a car ....

2 *ABOUT* YOU

Make questions to ask a friend. Use a–i in **1**.
Change some words.

a Can you cook Indian food? *Yes, I can / No, I can't.*
b Can you ride a horse? ....

More practice

Ask people to help me

Questions with **Can you?** and **Could you?**

Ask for help with *Can you? / Could you ...?*

1 Match situations a–e with sentences 1–5.

a You want your taxi driver to wait.

b Your suitcase is very heavy.

c You want to speak to the director. You ask her secretary.

d You want a short time to finish writing an email before you go to a meeting.

e You are at an information desk in a shopping mall.

1 Excuse me. Can you help me? I want to find a newsagent.

2 Can you tell me where your boss is?

3 Could you carry my bag, please?

4 Can you give me five more minutes?

5 Could you wait for me, please?

Can you tell me the time?

Could you pass me the salt?

2 Ask for help. Use the words in brackets.

a You want someone to open the window. (open)
Excuse me. Could you open the window, please?

b Your homework is very difficult. (help)
....

c You want the tomato ketchup. (pass)
....

d You need some money. You ask your friend. (lend)
....

e You want to look at a necklace in a shop. (show)
....

Ask for permission

Questions with **Can I?** and **Could I?**

Ask for permission with *Can I? / Could I ... ?*

Can I come in?

Can I borrow your car?

Could I speak to the manager, please?

Could I use this dictionary?

1 Complete the questions with the words in the box.

> ask ~~borrow~~ call have make

a Could I *borrow* five pounds, please?

b Can I .... a suggestion?

c Can I .... a question?

d Can I .... you later?

e Could I .... a biscuit?

2 What would you say?

a You want to borrow your friend's pen.
Can I borrow your pen, please?

b You want to look at your friend's homework answers.
....

c You want to take the last chocolate.
....

d You want to check your emails on your friend's computer.
....

e You want to ask your boss for permission to come to work late tomorrow.
....

More practice

I can ... Talk about habits, routines and repeated actions

Present Simple • statements

I go to the gym every day.

Monday Tuesday Wednesday Thursday Friday Saturday Sunday Monday Tuesday Wednesday Thursday Friday Saturday Sunday

> It's called the Present Simple – but the repeated action starts in the past and continues in the future!

He gives us a grammar test every month.

January February March April May June July August September October November December

I jog in the park every Tuesday morning.

🕐(a.m.)   🕐(a.m.)

Monday Tuesday Wednesday Thursday Friday Saturday Sunday Monday Tuesday Wednesday Thursday Friday Saturday Sunday

| I/You/We/They | play | golf at the |
| He/She/It | plays | weekends. |

+ s read→reads eat→eats
pay→pays see→sees

+ es catch→catches pass→passes
watch→watches discuss→discusses

y → + ies fly→flies try→tries
cry→cries carry→carries

⚠ have→has go→goes do→does

1 Write the correct verb form for *he/she/it*.

a write *writes*
b run
c catch
d fly
e do
f talk
g fry
h wash

i finish
j take
k cut
l copy
m undo
n try
o drive

2 Freya is a security guard at a shopping mall. Every day she does the same things. Complete the sentences with the correct form of the verbs in the box.

7:00 a.m   [talk unlock ~~switch~~ test]

a She *switches* the lights on.
b She _____ to the manager.
c She _____ the fire alarms.
d She _____ the doors.

All day   [call try watch walk]

e She _____ around.
f She _____ the customers.
g She _____ to help people.
h She _____ the police when there is a problem.

7:00 p.m.   [go say turn close]

i She _____ goodbye to the last customers.
j She _____ the doors.
k She _____ the lights off.
l She _____ home.

3 ABOUT YOU

What do you do every day? Write five sentences.

I get up at ...

More practice

I can ... Say how often things happen

Present Simple + adverbs of frequency

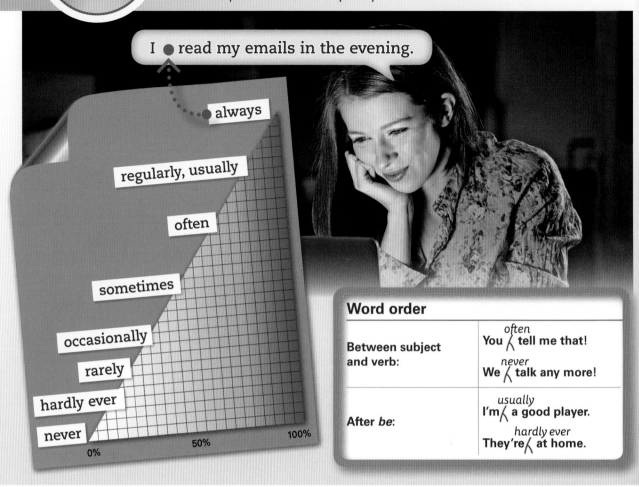

I ● read my emails in the evening.

always

regularly, usually

often

sometimes

occasionally

rarely

hardly ever

never

0% 50% 100%

Word order

Between subject and verb:	often You ∧ tell me that! never We ∧ talk any more!
After *be*:	usually I'm ∧ a good player. hardly ever They're ∧ at home.

1 Each sentence has one word in the wrong position. Correct it.

a I go always to the chess club on Tuesdays.

  I always go to the chess club on Tuesdays.

b I never am home before 10 p.m.

....

c We hardly do our homework ever.

....

d You cry when you usually watch a romantic film!

....

e She is at work often before anyone else.

....

f Never they make cakes for the school.

....

g He eats rarely vegetables.

....

2 ABOUT YOU

Write true sentences about yourself. Use a word from the box in each sentence.

> always ~~hardly ever~~ never occasionally
> often rarely sometimes usually

a play tennis

  I hardly ever play tennis.

b play computer games

....

c write long emails to my friends

....

d go out at the weekend

....

e talk on the phone for ages

....

f read a book before I go to sleep

....

g be late for school or work

....

More practice

Present Simple • time preposition **on**

I drive a van on Tuesdays and Wednesdays.

I'm a DJ on Monday evenings!

I teach in a nursery school on Friday mornings.

We go to a restaurant on 6th July every year – on our wedding anniversary!

on ...

Days of the week	Special days	Dates
on Monday / on Mondays	**on Mother's Day**	**on 1st March**
on Saturday / on Saturdays	**on my birthday**	**on December 26th**
	on Eid al-Fitr	**on Wednesday 5th October**
Parts of days	**on Christmas Day**	**on the 10th**
on Wednesday morning(s)		**on the last day of December**
on Sunday afternoon(s)		
on Friday evening(s)		

1 Complete the sentences. Say when things happen.

a
Jenny goes to her art class ...on Monday....

b
OK. We can meet ....

c
We usually go for a long walk ....

d
My daughter has dance class ....

e
Wednesday – Tennis
Ali always plays tennis ....

f
*Tues pm X
Tues Eve ✓*
I can't visit you .... , but I can come ....

g
OPEN Mon-Sat
The café isn't open ....

h
It's not fair! I don't want to go to school ....

2 *ABOUT* YOU

Write true sentences about your life.

a I usually .... on Friday evenings.

b I usually .... on New Year's Eve.

c I usually .... on Saturday.

d I never ....

in ...

Parts of the day	Years
in the morning	in 2010
in the afternoon	in 1879
in the evening	
	Seasons
Months	in (the) spring
in January	in (the) summer
in September	in (the) autumn
	in (the) winter

⚠ **on** ... See Unit 23

at ...

Times in the day	Periods of time
at midday	at the weekend*
at midnight	at Christmas
at 1 o'clock	at Easter
at 3.30	at Diwali
at 5.30	*US on the weekend
at half past three	

Times when things happen
at lunchtime
at break time
at sunrise
at sunset
at night

no preposition

Every ...
every Tuesday

This ...
this morning
this afternoon
~~this night~~ =
tonight

Yesterday, etc.
yesterday
tomorrow

1 Complete the sentences with *in* or *at*.

a We always come to this lake ..*in*.. spring.
b I usually visit my parents .... the weekend.
c When can we meet? Are you free ....Tuesday?
d I can't talk now. We can chat .... lunchtime.
e Please don't phone me .... midnight again!
f .... summer we often have a holiday by the sea.
g The dancing starts on West Hill .... sunrise.
h I was born .... 1996.
i I'm no good .... the morning! Talk to me .... break time!

2 Write the words in the correct columns.

on	in	at	no preposition
on Tuesdays			*every Friday*

a Tuesdays
b every Friday
c 2 o'clock
d lunchtime
e New Year's Day

f night
g yesterday
h the evening
i Wednesday evening
j this morning

k spring
l March
m 2001
n winter
o tonight

p the first day of January
q half past twelve
r the weekend

3 Match the sentence halves.

a Every week we visit Jason on
b The meeting always starts at
c The flower festival is in
d Her birthday party is on
e We work all week and then relax at

1 6th January.
2 the weekend.
3 Thursday afternoon.
4 2.30.
5 spring.

4 Complete each sentence with **one** word. (Different answers may be possible.)

a I buy a new coat ....*in*.... December every year.
b What do you usually do on .... afternoon?
c Let's go to the cinema .... !
d I have a Spanish lesson on ....
e We usually meet in ....
f When is the party? Is it on .... Day?
g When's your birthday? Is it in .... ?
h I've got a new job! I start on ....
i The postman usually comes at ....
j I always go to bed very late at ....
k I'm sorry. I can't meet you on ....

 **I can ...**

Talk about things that are generally true

Present Simple • statements

I teach History at the High School.

Past   Now   Future

I wear glasses.

We live in Geneva.

She speaks five languages.

They make computers.

Generally true (past, present and future)

I/You/We/They	work	in London.
He/She/It	work**s**	

+ s

We can talk about scientific (and other) facts:

The Moon goes round the Earth.

São Paolo in Brazil grows every year.

Giraffes sleep standing up.

1 Richard is talking about his restaurant. <u>Underline</u> the correct verb.

a I <u>own</u> / owns a small Italian restaurant in Manchester.

b Of course, we all *love / loves* pasta …

c … and our chef *cook / cooks* the best pasta in Britain!

d He *use / uses* the best fresh ingredients.

e The restaurant *open / opens* at lunchtime every day.

f We *close / closes* after midnight.

g We're very popular. Many people *write / writes* nice comments on the internet.

2 Look at the pictures. Write sentences about Judy. Use the verbs in the box.

drive   live   love   ~~speak~~   wear   work

a

b

She speaks three languages.
....
....

c

d

....
....

e

f **Fast Food Diner**

....
....

3 **INTERNET** QUIZ 🔍

<u>Underline</u> the correct ending for the sentences. If you don't know an answer, use the sentence beginnings to search the internet.

a Polar bears live in the *Arctic / Antarctic*.

b Water boils at *100° Celsius / 120° Celsius*.

c The Earth orbits *the Moon / the Sun*.

d Nocturnal animals sleep *during the night / during the day*.

e Koalas only eat *banana leaves / eucalyptus leaves*.

f Female black widow spiders sometimes eat *their mate / their parents*.

g Durian fruit smells like *perfume / feet*.

 More practice

I can ... Say what isn't true

Present Simple • negatives

(26)

I like spicy food.

don't
I ∧ like spicy food.

She likes spicy food.

doesn't
He ∧ likes spicy food.

I/You/We/They like		I/You/We/They don't like
He/She/It likes	→	He/She/It doesn't like

We can also make negatives with 'never'.
I always read books in Japanese. →
I never read books in Japanese.
They usually buy me chocolates for my birthday. →
They never buy me chocolates for my birthday.

1 Make the sentences negative.

a I live with my parents.
  I don't live with my parents.

b I like chocolate cake.

c She plays football on Wednesdays.

d The new printer works very well.

e Martin sings blues songs.

f I visit my grandparents at the weekend.

2 Look at the pictures. Make sentences with *don't* or *doesn't* and the words in the box.

> ~~agree with her~~ know the answer
> like ice cream open on Sundays
> speak English work

a

He doesn't agree with her.

b

c

d

e

f

3 INTERNET QUIZ

The facts are all wrong. Write new true sentences.
Use the internet to check anything you don't know.

a Sharks live in the mountains.
  Sharks don't live in the mountains. They live in the sea.

b The US President lives in Downing Street.

c Water freezes at 50° Celsius.

d Carrots grow on trees.

e The sun rises in the north.

f Mobile phones use wind power.

More practice

Present Simple • **yes/no** questions and short answers

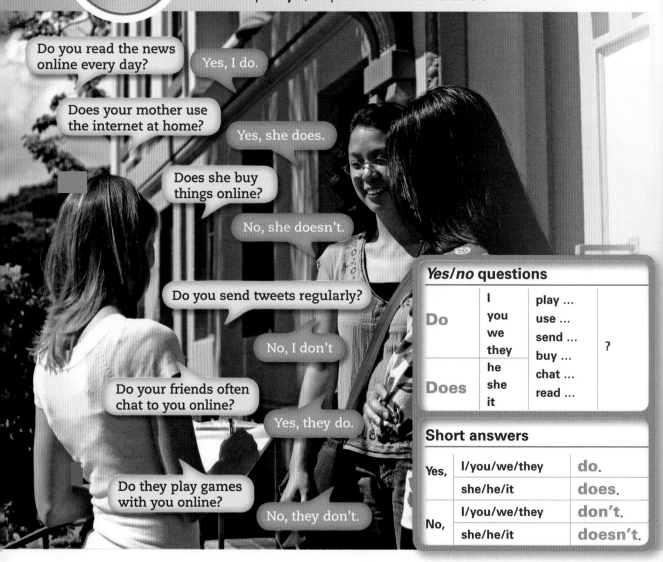

Do you read the news online every day?

Yes, I do.

Does your mother use the internet at home?

Yes, she does.

Does she buy things online?

No, she doesn't.

Do you send tweets regularly?

No, I don't

Do your friends often chat to you online?

Yes, they do.

Do they play games with you online?

No, they don't.

Yes/no questions

Do	I you we they	play ... use ... send ... buy ...	?
Does	he she it	chat ... read ...	

Short answers

Yes,	I/you/we/they	**do**.
	she/he/it	**does**.
No,	I/you/we/they	**don't**.
	she/he/it	**doesn't**.

---

1 Write *do* or *does*.

Fitness Quiz

a _Do_ you eat five pieces of fruit every day?

b _____ you sleep more than eight hours at night?

c _____ you swim every week?

d _____ your mum jog?

e _____ your best friend do sport regularly?

f _____ you go to bed before 10 p.m.?

g _____ your colleagues walk up and down stairs?

h _____ you get up before 7.00 in the morning?

i _____ you eat a lot of fast food?

j _____ your doctor think you are healthy?

2 **ABOUT YOU**

Write *Yes, I do/No, I don't*, etc. Give true answers.

a Do you live on Mars? _No, I don't._

b Do you live in Latin America? ....

c Does your best friend live near you? ....

d Do you play volleyball? ....

e Do you like chocolate? ....

f Does your teacher give you homework? ....

g Do you cook every day? ....

h Do your friends enjoy dance music? ....

i Does your father regularly read a newspaper? ....

j Do you know how to play the piano? ....

k Do you watch a lot of TV? ....

3 Think of some more *do/does* questions (like **2**) that you could ask a friend.

Do you ...

More practice

Present Simple • **Wh**- questions

> **We can put *Wh*- question words in front of *do/does* questions.**

Where does she go to school?

Who does he look like?

Why do you come to this gym?

How often do you cook pizza for lunch?

How much does it cost?

What do they want to eat?

Do/Does ...? questions have short answers: *yes/no/sometimes.*

Wh- ... *do/does ...?* questions have longer answers that give more information.

	Do you play football?	Yes, I do.
When ...	do you play football?	On Tuesday evening.
Where ...		At the youth club.
Why ...		Because I love the game!
How often ...		Every week.
Who ...	do you play football with?	Girls from my town.
What ...	other games do you play?	I really enjoy tennis.

Some common questions

Where do you come from?		What is your hometown/country/nationality?
What do you think?	=	What is your opinion?
What do you do?		What is your job?
How much does it cost?		What is the price?

1 Match questions a–h with answers 1–8.

a Where do you come from?

b How much does it cost?

c What do you think about his idea?

d When do you take a break?

e Why do you live here?

f Who do you work with?

g What do you want to eat?

h How do you feel?

1 I don't like it.

2 I have a brilliant team.

3 Mexico.

4 Pizza, please!

5 $10.

6 Wonderful! I feel great!

7 At 2 o'clock.

8 Because it's a lovely town.

2 Frank is only 23 – but he's a millionaire! Write Sam's questions using the words in brackets.

Sam Where ..*do you live*.. [a] (you/live)?

Frank In California – in a beautiful house on a beach!

Sam Where .... [b] (you/work)?

Frank In San Francisco.

Sam What .... [c] (your company/make)?

Frank Computer memory sticks. We sell millions of them!

Sam Why .... [d] (your customers/ like) them?

Frank They're small and very pretty!

Sam How often .... [e] (you/go) to the office?

Frank Maybe three times a month.

Sam What .... [f] (you/do) every day?

Frank Well ... I play tennis every day ... and swim.

Sam What .... [g] (you/enjoy) most in your life?

Frank Very good coffee!

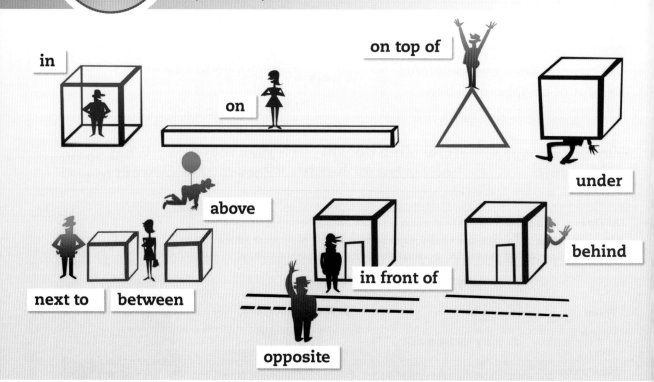

1 Where are the people? Complete the sentences.

A is _on top of the school._

B is ....

C is ....

D is ....

E is ....

F is ....

G is ....

2 This is Red Square in Moscow. Complete the sentences.

a The GUM department store (9) is _opposite_ the Kremlin wall (3).

b The Mausoleum (6) is .... the Kremlin wall (3).

c The Kremlin (1) is .... the Kremlin wall (3).

d The Spasskaya tower (2) is .... the Mausoleum (6).

e St Basil's Cathedral (4) is .... the museum (7).

f There's a statue (5) .... St Basil's Cathedral (4).

g The Mausoleum (6) is .... St Basil's (4) and the museum (7).

h There's a Metro station (8) .... the museum (7).

More practice

Present Progressive • statements

Use the Present Progressive to talk about something that is happening at this moment, **now**.

I	'm/am		
You/We/They	're/are	read**ing**	a book.
He/She/It	's/is		

You need TWO verbs: *be* AND a main verb

The Present Progressive is also called the Present Continuous.

I'm writing an email to Fred.

We're going into a tunnel!

Jake's telling her the truth!

She's wearing a very expensive new dress.

You're joking!

The dog's feeling ill.

They're playing golf.

1 Tick (✓) the sentences that are about something that is happening right now.

a We are flying at a height of 100,000 metres. ✓
b The first cars are coming round the corner. ....
c I read lots of books about history. ....
d It's snowing! ....
e I'm waiting! ....

2 Look at the pictures and complete the sentences. Use the verbs in the box in the correct form.

bark   cook   laugh   rain   ~~sing~~   talk

a

She 's singing.

b

He ....

c

We ....

d

It ....

e

They ....

f

It ....

3 Complete the sentences. Use the verbs in brackets in the Present Progressive.

a The traffic is awful today. We *'re going* very slowly! (go)
b I don't usually have breakfast, but this morning I .... eggs! (cook)
c A lion .... in the road near the zoo! (walk)
d The police .... to the athletes in the sports hall. (talk)
e It's freezing today! I .... a scarf, gloves and a woolly hat. (wear)
f Andrea .... with the other children. (play)

4 ABOUT YOU

What are you doing **now**? Tick (✓) the true sentences. Put a cross (✗) if it is not true.

a I'm studying English. ....
b I'm listening to music. ....
c I'm eating chocolate. ....
d I'm thinking about grammar. ....
e I'm working very hard. ....

Write three more **true** sentences about what you are doing now.

f *I'm* ....
g ....
h ....

Make -ing endings correctly

Present participles

Most verbs just add -ing

forget → forgetting

walk → walking

The -ing form of the verb is called the present participle.

If the verb ends with consonant/vowel/consonant, double the final consonant

If the verb ends with a single 'e', lose the 'e'

take → taking

If the verb ends with 'ie, change 'ie' to 'y'

tie → tying

 w, x, y: grow → growing, fix → fixing, play → playing. Also NB: visit → visiting, enter → entering

1 What is the -ing form of the verbs?

a sing   *singing*
b watch   ....
c use   ....
d write   ....
e smoke   ....
f cut   ....
g build   ....
h bake   ....
i stay   ....
j laugh   ....
k stop   ....
l go   ....

2 Complete the sentences. Use the verbs in brackets.

a I'm ...*cooking*... some rice for supper. (cook)
b Natalie's over there. She's .... to Michel. (chat)
c Look! Keira's .... four suitcases! (take)
d That's not true! I think he's .... (lie)
e I'm .... the soup. (heat)
f She's .... my new pen. (use)
g This road is .... worse. (get)

Avoid unnecessary repetition

Present Progressive • omission of repeated verbs

When we have more than one Present Progressive verb, we don't need to repeat the subject or auxiliary verb.

She's sitting in the lounge and she's eating chocolate cake and she's watching TV. ▶ She's sitting in the lounge, eating chocolate cake and watching TV.

1 Make the sentences shorter.

a Sara is reading a book and Sara is checking her dictionary.
Sara is reading a book and checking her dictionary.

b The children are singing and the children are dancing and the children are laughing.
....

c That's dangerous. You are running and you are eating at the same time!

d Wilga is doing her homework and Wilga is playing a computer game!
....

e I'm sitting in my car and I'm waiting for George.
....

f Hello! Can anyone hear me? I'm standing outside your front door and I'm trying to get in and I'm pressing all the buttons but the door doesn't open! Hello?
....

More practice

Present Progressive • statements

What do you think?

Use the Present Progressive to write messages about what you are doing now.

Is it OK to send a text message to your friends when ...

a you're watching a film in the cinema?

b you're talking to a customer?

c you're doing a grammar exercise in class?

d you're having a romantic meal with your boyfriend/girlfriend?

e you're driving?

1 Look at the pictures. What message is each person sending their friends? Use the words in brackets. (Some of these people aren't telling the truth!)

a (walk/beach)

I'm walking on the beach.

b (run/work)

c (work/home)

d (rob/bank)

e (meet/customer)

f (fly/Rio)

2 You have a lot of text messages from your friends. Some of them contain mistakes. Tick (✓) if the message is correct. Put a cross (✗) if it's wrong — and correct the mistake.

a I'm ~~drink~~ tea with students from my group.

    ✗ *drinking*

b We all listening to the radio news.

c I'm working on my computer.

d I playing chess with my brother.

e Rosa and Elena is working at home today.

f The girl are singing a lovely song.

Present Progressive • meaning: temporary, around now

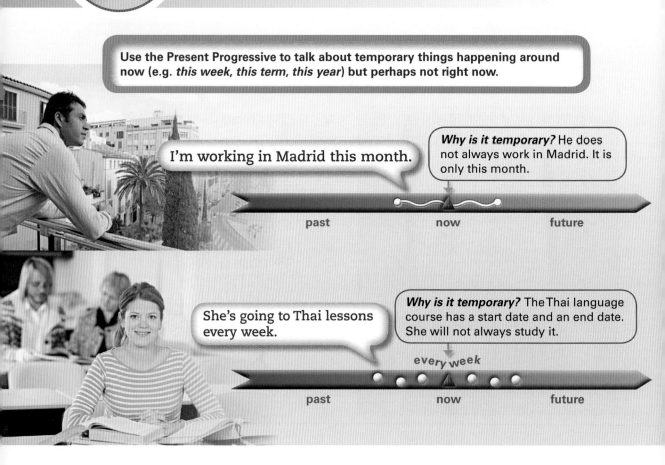

Use the Present Progressive to talk about temporary things happening around now (e.g. *this week, this term, this year*) but perhaps not right now.

I'm working in Madrid this month.

Why is it temporary? He does not always work in Madrid. It is only this month.

past   now   future

She's going to Thai lessons every week.

Why is it temporary? The Thai language course has a start date and an end date. She will not always study it.

every week

past   now   future

1 Complete the sentences.

a I usually work in the Sales department, but this month I *'m working* in Marketing.

b I usually listen to rock music, but today I .... to Beethoven!

c Josh usually eats a lot of fast food, but this week he .... salad every day!

d Sue usually grows vegetables in her garden, but this year she .... flowers.

e When he comes to England, Fred usually stays with his mum, but this time he .... with friends in London.

f Marie usually makes clothes for children, but this week she .... wedding dresses!

2 THE TOUGH ONE

Complete the sentences. Think about which verbs you could use!

a I usually drive to work, but this week I .... to work.

b Polly usually plays football every day, but this week she .... to the gym instead.

c Martin and Kirsty usually book a hotel near the beach, but this time they .... with friends.

3 Amina is writing an email to her friend Corbin. Complete the email with the verbs in brackets.

From: Amina
To: Corbin337
Subject: Hi

Hello Corbin,
Yes – I am at university now! This year I *'m living* ᵃ (live) in Berlin! I .... ᵇ (share) an apartment with two Estonian friends. All three of us .... ᶜ (study) Archaeology. It's really interesting. We .... ᵈ (take) three extra options as well: English, IT skills and first aid. I .... ᵉ (work) very hard, but I think that I .... ᶠ (fail) the IT course! Life in Berlin is very expensive, but I .... ᵍ (save) some money so that I can buy a plane ticket to visit you soon!

More practice

Present Progressive • future meaning

Use the Present Progressive to talk about future events that have already been planned or arranged.

I planned or arranged it then.

It will happen in the future.

past   now   future

How can we know if a Present Progressive sentence is about the future?

We're travelling to Buenos Aires **next month.** ← future time reference

I'm meeting Jorge for **lunch.** ← an event which suggests a time

Some sentences could be about either now or the future. Think about the meaning of the <u>whole conversation</u> to decide which meaning is correct.

We're staying at a lovely hotel in London.

Jess: You're going on holiday next week, aren't you?

Pia: Yes, we're staying at a lovely hotel in London.

---

1 Which sentences are: about 'now' (N); about the future (F)?

a Listen! I think the train's coming in.   N

b We're flying to Delhi next week.

c Shhh! The show's starting.

d They are getting married in spring.

e Sorry. I can't come to lunch tomorrow. I'm visiting my uncle.

f I'm meeting the project team at 3.00.

g I'm finishing my lunch.

h The representatives are arriving in the morning.

i I'm having a party on my birthday. Will you come?

---

2 Look at Yi's diary for next week. Write what he's doing each day.

June	week no 23
a Saturday	go cinema 7 p.m.
b Sunday	play football 2 p.m.
c Monday	meet Thai visitors 10 a.m.
d Tuesday	fly to Rome 6.25 a.m.
e Wednesday	present the company's new products to the Italian team
f Thursday	fly back
g Friday	report to the CEO and the board

a *On Saturday evening he's going to the cinema.*

b ....

c ....

d ....

e ....

f ....

g ....

3 **ABOUT YOU**

Write what you are doing next week.

a On Monday I ....

b On ....

c At the weekend ....

36 I can ... Make an excuse about why I can't do something

Present Progressive • excuses

Use the Present Progressive to say why you can't do something in the future.
Make an excuse by explaining what you have already arranged.

| Say 'sorry' | then | Say what you can't do | then | Say what you have already planned to do. |

For example: *Sorry. I can't help you with the project tomorrow. I'm driving to Birmingham for the day.*

What do you think?

Do you think these are good or terrible excuses?

a Sorry. I can't meet you at two. I'm seeing my boss then.

b Sorry. We can't go on holiday in May. I'm taking some important exams then.

c I really want to go on a diet, but I'm starting a cookery course next week.

d I'm so sorry. I would love to have a meal with you, but I'm meeting my boyfriend at 7.

e Sorry. I can't go shopping with you because I'm washing my hair this afternoon.

1 Complete the excuses. Use the verbs in the box in the Present Progressive.

> catch   drive   fly   leave
> teach   ~~meet~~   work

a Sorry. I can't see you now. I *'m meeting* a client.

b Sorry. I can't come to your party. I .... to New Zealand next week!

c Sorry. I can't help you with your homework. I .... a bus at half past six.

d Sorry. I can't go shopping tonight. I .... Josh to the doctor.

e Sorry. I can't do the marketing project with you next Monday. Teresa and I .... already .... together all next week.

f Sorry. I can't make breakfast for the children. I .... for the office in a few minutes!

g Sorry. I can't meet you at 3 p.m. I .... two classes this afternoon.

2 Think of some good excuses to explain why you can't do things.

a Sorry. I'll be two hours late for work tomorrow. I *'m meeting an important client.*............

b Sorry. Mila won't be at the meeting tomorrow. She ....

c Sorry. Yosip can't come to your party tomorrow. He ....

d Sorry. I can't play tennis tomorrow. I ....

e I wish I could help you with the report, but this afternoon I ....

More practice

I can ...
Make Present Progressive negatives and questions

37

Present Progressive • negatives and questions

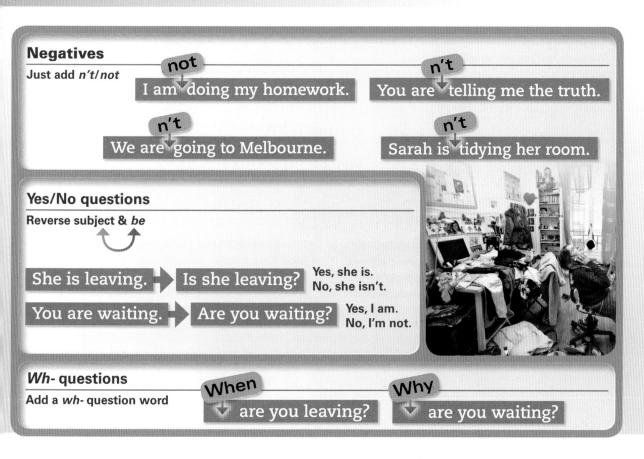

Negatives
Just add *n't/not*

not → I am doing my homework.

n't → You are telling me the truth.

n't → We are going to Melbourne.

n't → Sarah is tidying her room.

Yes/No questions
Reverse subject & *be*

She is leaving. → Is she leaving? — Yes, she is. No, she isn't.

You are waiting. → Are you waiting? — Yes, I am. No, I'm not.

Wh- questions
Add a *wh*- question word

When ↓ are you leaving?

Why ↓ are you waiting?

---

1 Make the sentences negative.

a They're coming this evening.
They aren't coming this evening.

b We're doing very well in the tests.

c The children are playing computer games.

d I'm cooking supper again tonight.

e The engine is starting.

f It's snowing in Saudi Arabia!

g The teacher's waiting for Amir.

2 Write the questions.

a what / Albert / do
What's Albert doing?
He's painting the kitchen.

b Vicki / meet / the visitors

Yes, she is.

c why / the children / sing

They're practising for the show.

d our plane / leave / soon

No. It's delayed by two hours.

e I / pronounce / this word / correctly

Yes. You're saying it very well.

f where / the players / go

To their coach.

g you / get / a new car

No. I don't have enough money.

More practice

I can ...

Remember which verbs aren't usually used in the Present Progressive

Active and stative verbs

There are some verbs that we don't usually use in the Present Progressive. We use the Present Simple instead.

I'm liking this film. ✗

She's believing in aliens. ✗

Karuna is loving cheese sandwiches. ✗

He's wanting a new car. ✗

Yes. I'm knowing the way. ✗

I am believing you. ➡ I <u>believe</u> you.

They are knowing the answer. ➡ They <u>know</u> the answer.

The boys are liking the new books. ➡ The boys <u>like</u> the new books.

This cake is tasting delicious. ➡ This cake <u>tastes</u> delicious.

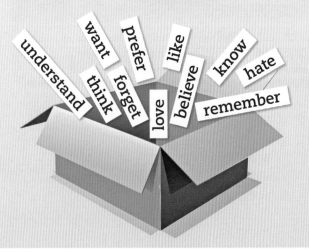

understand, want, think, prefer, forget, love, like, believe, know, remember, hate

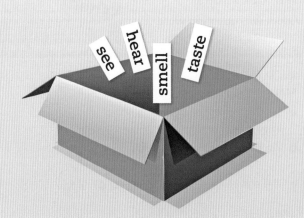

see, hear, smell, taste

1 <u>Underline</u> the correct words.

a Oh, thank you so much for the present! <u>I love</u> / I'm loving this necklace.

b That's an easy question. I know / I'm knowing the answer!

c I enjoy / I'm enjoying this book.

d I believe / I'm believing that most people are honest.

e Please don't be angry. I tell / I'm telling you the truth!

f The girl with the long red hair? Yes, I remember / I'm remembering her name.

g Let me look at your computer. I understand / I'm understanding the problem.

h This soup tastes / is tasting delicious.

2 Complete the sentences. Use Present Progressive or Present Simple and the verbs in brackets.

a He ..'s watching.... that war film again. He really ....likes........ it! (watch/like)

b She .... your problem and she .... to help. (understand/try)

c Don't worry! I .... the directions! I .... where to go. (remember/know)

d I .... this flat! This room .... horrible! (hate/smell)

e Oh dear! The baby .... again. He .... some food. (cry/want)

f Hiro .... his guitar. I .... he plays really well. (love/think)

More practice

Decide whether to use Present Simple or Present Progressive

I can ...

39

Present Simple compared with Present Progressive

We usually use the Present Simple for habits, routines and things that are generally or always true.
We use the Present Progressive for things happening now.

Present Simple

every day, always, usually, generally, sometimes

Present Simple: habits, routines, always true

past   now   future

Pete works at the garage.

Leaves fall in autumn.

I live in Durban.

I enjoy chocolate cakes!

Present Progressive

right now, around now, temporary

Present Progressive: now or around now

past   now   future

Pete's working at the garage.

The leaves are falling.

I'm living in Montreal.

I'm enjoying this carrot cake!

---

1 Which sentences are about something that is: generally, usually or always true (G); happening now or around now (N)?

a She always goes to the nightclub on Fridays. ___G___
b He's changing the light bulb. ....
c She writes very good English. ....
d We're renting a flat in Montevideo. ....
e Polar bears live in the Arctic. ....
f I'm writing a birthday card for Emma. ....

2 <u>Underline</u> the correct words.

a She's good at languages. <u>*She speaks*</u> / *She's speaking* Chinese and Russian.

b Their home is in Vietnam – but this month *they stay* / *they're staying* in Paris.

c I want to keep fit so *I always go* / *I'm always going* to the gym every Tuesday.

d Is there anything you want? *Mahmoud writes* / *Mahmoud's writing* a shopping list.

e *I usually write* / *I'm usually writing* my blog every evening. In fact, *I blog* / *I'm blogging* now!

f Seb and Olga are both doing a course this month. *He studies* / *He's studying* Business and Marketing and *she does* / *she's doing* Economics.

g *Matteo texts* / *Matteo's texting* all our friends about tonight's party.

3 Read about Jerzy. Then answer the questions.

> Jerzy is a pianist. He lives in Hollywood. This month he's in Warsaw. It's 10 o'clock at night. He isn't playing music now. He's in a restaurant with his girlfriend, Rosie. She's a dancer. Rosie is having dessert. Jerzy is saying 'I like dessert — but I don't want any today. I want a coffee.'

a Does Jerzy play the piano?
b Is Jerzy playing the piano?
c Does he live in Warsaw?
d Is Rosie a dancer?
e Does Rosie dance?
f Is Rosie dancing?
g Does Jerzy enjoy dessert?

4 THE TOUGH ONE

Answer the questions.

a You are a writer. You are sitting at home writing your book. Someone phones you and says 'What are you doing?' What is your reply?

b You are a writer. You are talking to a new friend. He asks 'What do you do?' What is your reply?

c A thief is in an empty room at a party, stealing money from handbags! A man comes into the room. Does he ask (i) 'What do you do?' or (ii) 'What are you doing?'

More practice

47

was and *were*

Were you at school yesterday afternoon?

No. I was at the dentist!

Was it OK?

No, it wasn't! It was awful!

Where was the concert?

In a park in London.

Was it expensive?

No, it was free.

Was it good?

Yes, it was! Maroon 5 were fantastic.

Were Peter and Marta there?

No, they weren't. But Sean was. And his brother was there, too.

	now	past
I	am →	was (wasn't)
He/She/It	is →	was (wasn't)
You/We/They	are →	were (weren't)

Yes/No questions

Was	I/he/she/it	the winner?
Were	you/we/they	the winners?

Short answers

Yes, I/he/she/it was.	No, I/he/she/it wasn't.
Yes, you/we/they were.	No, you/we/they weren't.

***Wh-* questions**

Wh- + *was/were*

Where was the race?
When was the meeting?
Why were the children late?
What were the correct answers?

2 Answer the questions using the words in brackets.

a Why wasn't Petra at work yesterday? (ill)
  She was ill.

b Where was John this morning? (meeting)

c Where was the football match? (Italy)

d Why were you late? (traffic jam)

e How much was your new bag? ($39)

f Was it a good concert? (boring)

1 Complete the sentences with *am/is/are* or *was/were*.

a The weather ......*was*...... terrible yesterday. There ......*was*...... a huge storm.

b Oh, I love this song. Adele ...*is*... my favourite singer.

c There .... so many people at last night's meeting. It .... very noisy.

d There .... only three chocolates left! Would you like one?

e When the exam finished we .... all very happy.

f When I .... ten years old I .... mad about ballet. My dance teachers .... very good.

g When .... our last meeting? .... all of you here?

3 **INTERNET QUIZ** 🔍

Use the internet to find the answers and underline the correct verb.

a .... and .... *was / were* the first two men on the moon.

b .... *was / were* the director of the film *Life of Pi*.

c Kyoto *was / were* the old capital city of ....

d Shakespeare *was / were* .... years old when he died.

e In 1930 .... *was / were* the first country to win the football World Cup.

More practice 🌐

Past Simple • regular verbs

Regular verb + -ed

look → looked   talk → talked   want → wanted

walk → walked   play → played

stayed → cleaned → cooked → finished → washed → waited → started → painted

e: like → liked   race → raced   close → closed   believe → believed

nsonant + y: study → studied   hurry → hurried   try → tried

x2: hop → hopped   rob → robbed   travel → travelled   stop → stopped

---

1 Write the Past Simple form of the verbs.

a walk _____walked_____   f try _____   j remember _____   n fry _____
b cough _____   g follow _____   k play _____   o jog _____
c wait _____   h taste _____   l carry _____   p push _____
d watch _____   i jump _____   m save _____   q travel _____
e sign _____

2 Use verbs from **1** to complete the sentences.

a The children _____played_____ with their new toys for hours.

b We _____ TV all evening.

c She _____ the fish in vegetable oil.

d The dog _____ over the gate and _____ Jack down the road.

e The burger _____ horrible.

f Bea _____ her name on the application form.

g The porter _____ my suitcases up to my hotel room.

h I suddenly _____ that it was my girlfriend's birthday.

3 Number the sentences to make a story.

a She finished, looked at me, then walked to the window and jumped out. _____

b I watched her drink all the milk. _____

c I looked inside. A cat jumped out! _____

d When I opened it, there was no one there. _____

e She never visited me again. And I never discovered who packed her in that box. _____

f Last week someone knocked loudly on my front door. __1__

g But there was a strange box outside my door. _____

h I placed her on the floor. She tasted the milk and liked it. _____

i She looked frightened. I picked her up and walked back into the apartment. _____

j I carried her to the kitchen and filled a bowl with milk. _____

More practice

49

Regular + -ed	**Irregular** **No -ed! Many different forms!**

grow → grew
blow → blew
know → knew
fly → flew
draw → drew
throw → threw

run → ran
begin → began
drink → drank
sing → sang
ring → rang
swim → swam

wear → wore
tear → tore

write → wrote
drive → drove
ride → rode
rise → rose

get → got
forget → forgot

take → took
understand → understood
stand → stood

keep → kept
sleep → slept
creep → crept
feel → felt
leave → left
build → built
burn → burnt
learn → learnt
lose → lost

buy → bought
bring → brought
catch → caught
think → thought
fight → fought
teach → taught

wake → woke
speak → spoke
break → broke

steal → stole

sell → sold
tell → told

dig → dug
win → won

Important ones!

go → went
do → did
have → had
say → said

come → came
become → became

see → saw
eat → ate
make → made
find → found
give → gave
hear → heard
tell → told
meet → met

No change!

put → put
let → let
hit → hit
cost → cost
cut → cut
shut → shut

Same spelling! Different pronunciation!

read → read

1 Write the Past Simple form of the verbs. (Some are regular!)

a	see	_saw_	**h** turn	
b	fly		**i** open	
c	drive		**j** speak	
d	draw		**k** meet	
e	climb		**l** race	
f	leave		**m** read	
g	go		**n** write	

2 Read the texts about Bryan and Sally. Rewrite them about yesterday.

a

Bryan makes a new cake every day. When he finishes, he gets into his car and drives to the club. He puts the cake on the table and asks everyone to have some. When they taste it, they all say that it is delicious.

Bryan made a new cake yesterday. When he ...

b

Sally goes to the gym every day. She swims for 30 minutes and then does exercises for another half an hour. After that she feels tired! She has a quick shower and changes into her work clothes. She goes out and catches the bus to her office. She works until 5 p.m. and then jogs all the way home! She eats a healthy supper, switches on the TV and watches the news. Not surprisingly, she falls asleep in the chair!

Sally went to the gym yesterday. She ...

3 Complete the story with the verbs in brackets in the Past Simple.

Sir Lancelot _bought_ ᵃ (buy) a new sword. Then he _____ ᵇ (put on) his armour, _____ ᶜ (climb) onto his horse and _____ ᵈ (ride) out of the castle. He _____ ᵉ (leave) the city and _____ ᶠ (go) deep into the forest. Suddenly he _____ ᵍ (hear) a dragon near him. He _____ ʰ (get off) his horse and _____ ⁱ (walk) towards the sound. He _____ ʲ (feel) nervous. The knight _____ ᵏ (creep) past some rocks and _____ ˡ (see) the dragon. It _____ ᵐ (be) outside a dark cave. The princess _____ ⁿ (stand) opposite the dragon, smiling. In her hand she _____ ᵒ (have) a cup of tea. She _____ ᵖ (notice) Lancelot. 'Hello!' she _____ ۹ (say). 'Come over! Would you like some tea? This lovely dragon just _____ ʳ (tell) me a wonderful story about his family.'

4 INTERNET QUIZ

The verbs in the sentences are mixed up. Correct them. Use the internet to help you.

a Karl Marx sang *Das Kapital* in 1867. _wrote_

b Rontgen built the Nobel Prize in 1901 for his discovery of X-rays. _____

c On 17th December 1903 Wilbur and Orville Wright walked for the first time. _____

d In 1815 Napoleon and Wellington flew the Battle of Waterloo. _____

e John F Kennedy met the President of the USA in 1961. _____

f Neil Armstrong ~~wrote~~ on the Moon in 1969. _____

g 1n 1962 The Beatles fought on TV for the first time. _____

h The Aztecs won many pyramids in Central America between the fourteenth and sixteenth centuries. _____

i Thomas Stafford and Alexei Leonov became in space on July 15th 1975. _____

Past Simple • **yes/no** questions

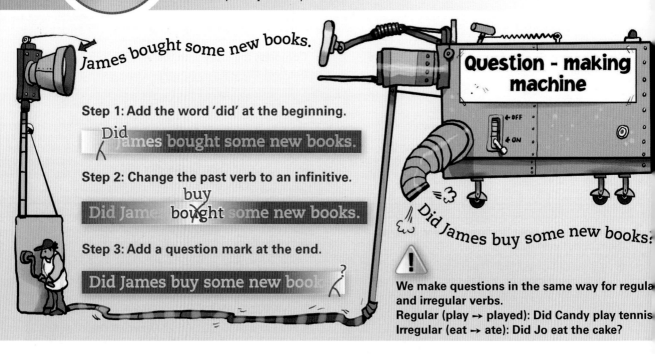

James bought some new books.

Step 1: Add the word 'did' at the beginning.

Did James bought some new books.

Step 2: Change the past verb to an infinitive.

buy
Did James bought some new books.

Step 3: Add a question mark at the end.

Did James buy some new books?

Question - making machine

Did James buy some new books?

⚠️ We make questions in the same way for regular and irregular verbs.
Regular (play → played): Did Candy play tennis?
Irregular (eat → ate): Did Jo eat the cake?

1 Use the question-making machine to make questions from the sentences.

a Ben wanted an ice cream.
Did Ben want an ice cream?

b Rita and Pepe painted the house.

c She went to Dubai.

d They had a nice lunch together.

e Rihanna sang all evening.

f He made a nice meal.

2 Read the questions and answers. Complete the questions with the correct verb form.

a Q: Did you ___*like*___ the museum?
A: Yes, I liked it very much.

b Q: Did the children _____ the science programme yesterday?
A: Yes, they watched it last night.

c Q: Did Max _____ the chips?
A: Yes, he ate all of them!

d Q: Did Dorota _____ to the USA?
A: Yes, she went to Washington DC.

e Q: Did you _____ a new mouse?
A: Yes, I bought one yesterday.

f Q: Did the boys _____ a good party?
A: Yes, they had a very noisy party!

3 Match the questions with the pictures.

a Did you change your mind?   3
b Did you remember your sandwiches?   ....
c Did you find that website?   ....
d Did you have a good journey?   ....
e Did you tell him?   ....

More practice

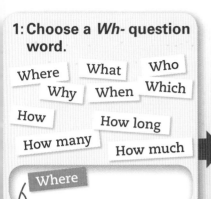
THE QUESTION FACTORY

1: Choose a *Wh-* question word.

Where   What   Who
Why   When   Which
How   How long
How many   How much

⟨ Where

➤

2: Add *did* after the *Wh-* word.

⟨ did

➤

**3: Finish the question. BUT ...
Use an infinitive (NOT a past verb).**

~~you went?~~   ⟨ you go?

⬇

Where did you go?

---

1 Make questions using the 'question factory'.

a	Amina bought something.	What?	*What did she buy?*
b	She saw something.	What?	
c	Jan wrote something.	What?	
d	He met someone.	Who?	
e	They sang something.	What?	
f	They went somewhere.	Where?	
g	She did something.	What?	
h	He laughed.	Why?	
i	She took one book.	Which?	
j	They made a lot of cakes.	How many?	
k	They left.	Why?	

---

2 Tom has lost a box full of cash. He is in his boss's office. Put the words in the correct order to make her questions.

Come in, Tom! So ...

a you what lose did ? *What did you lose?*
b when happen it did ? ....
c why the you did box have ? ....
d much it have money how did ? ....
e help did you ask who for ? ....
f did look where you ? ....
g search long did how you ? ....

Two hours later, Tom finds the cash box. His boss asks:

h you did it where find ? ....
i did it you how find ? ....

---

3 a Use the word pool to write six questions.

b What is the longest question you can make?

what   how   where   why
who   did   your   meet
father   go   eat   you
the   magician   make   dinner
rabbit   cake   long   last
a   cook   to   ?
for   Rome   night   in

I can ...

Give short answers about the past

Past Simple • short answers

Did you go to the match?

Did your team win?

Yes, I did.

No, they didn't!

Yes,	I/you/he/she/it/we/they	did.
No,	I/you/he/she/it/we/they	didn't.

1 ✓ = Answer 'yes'. ✗ = Answer 'no'.

a Did your family go to the concert?   ✗ *No, they didn't.*

b Did Ruth pass her driving test?   ✓

c Did Lucas eat breakfast this morning?   ✗

d Did Neil Armstrong walk on the moon?   ✓

e Did Edward listen to that Coldplay song?   ✗

f Did the dog eat its food?   ✓

g Did Susan watch TV this morning?   ✗

2 **ABOUT YOU**

Give true answers about yourself.

a Did you buy a new Porsche this morning?   *No, I didn't.*

b Did you have a long walk this morning?

c Did you have a shower last night?

d Did you phone anyone yesterday?

e Did you watch the news on TV at breakfast?

I can ...

Say what didn't happen in the past

Past Simple • negatives

We went to the supermarket last night.

1 Use *didn't*.

2 Use the infinitive (not the Past Simple).

didn't   go

We ⋀ went ⋀ to the supermarket last night.

1 Use the verb in brackets to complete each sentence with a positive and a negative.

a I __spoke__ to Billy, but I __didn't speak__ to Julia. (speak)

b I _____ the Statue of Liberty, but I _____ Times Square. (see)

c I _____ to São Paolo, but I _____ to Rio. (go)

d I _____ the computer, but I _____ the TV. (break)

e I _____ Josie, but I _____ Marty. (tell)

2 Write negative sentences about Andrew using the words in brackets.

a Andrew drove to work. (✗ the shops)
He didn't drive to the shops.

b Andrew listened to a CD. (✗ the radio)

c Andrew parked in the car park. (✗ on the street)

d Andrew ran to his office. (✗ the café)

e Andrew talked to his colleague. (✗ boss)

f Andrew felt happy. (✗ sad)

More practice

Past Simple + **when/then/after/before**

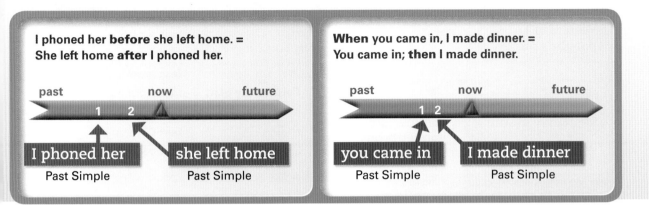

I phoned her **before** she left home. =
She left home **after** I phoned her.

past	now	future
1	**2**	

I phoned her
Past Simple

she left home
Past Simple

When you came in, I made dinner. =
You came in; **then** I made dinner.

past	now	future
1 2		

you came in
Past Simple

I made dinner
Past Simple

1 Which action happened first? **X** or **Y**?

	X	Y	
a	I read the book	after you told me about it.	*Y*
b	I went to the shops	and then had a coffee.	*X*
c	When he arrived,	everyone sang 'Happy Birthday'.	....

	X	Y	
d	You felt bored	before you watched the film.	....
e	I planted some flowers	after the rain stopped.	....
f	When the baby cried,	Dad ran over to the bed.	....
g	We crossed the road	and then walked in the park.	....

2 Read what Jenny did yesterday afternoon. Write *after* or *before* in the sentences.

 leave house

 catch bus

 arrive at town centre

 buy some chocolate

 meet Gyles

 walk to theatre

 watch *Guys and Dolls*

 have a coffee

 say goodbye to Gyles, catch bus home

 arrive home

a Jenny caught a bus to the town centre ten minutes ....*after*.... she left her house.

b Jenny left home 45 minutes .... she met Gyles.

c Jenny bought some chocolate .... she met Gyles.

d .... she met Gyles, they both went to the theatre.

e .... they left the theatre, Gyles and Jenny had a coffee.

f Jenny had a coffee with Gyles .... she caught a bus home.

g She arrived home fifteen minutes .... she said goodbye to Gyles.

3 Rewrite the sentences starting with *When*.

a The bell rang. Everyone left the building.
   When the bell rang, everyone left the building.

b The bus stopped. Susie got off.
   ....

c I moved to Canada after I lost my job in England.
   ....

d The police rushed to the bank after they heard the alarm.
   ....

e The car made a loud noise. The baby woke up.
   ....

f I tried to phone you after I got your email.
   ....

More practice

I can ...

Say when things happened

Past Simple • time expressions

Yesterday I bought a puppy.

Yesterday afternoon we all went to the café.

Sheila rang me **yesterday morning.**

Tommy came home **the day before yesterday.**

I visited my gran

last week.
last weekend.
last month.
last summer.
last winter.
last Christmas.
last year.

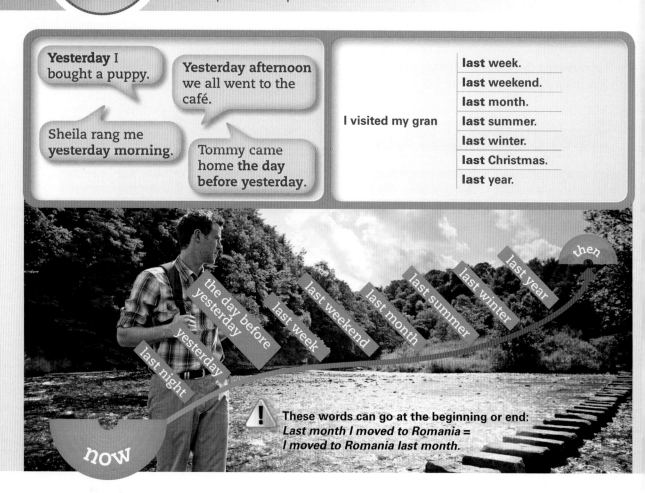

These words can go at the beginning or end:
*Last month I moved to Romania =
I moved to Romania last month.*

1 Read the information. Then complete the sentences with the time expressions in the box.

> ~~last month~~   last night   last weekend
> last year   the day before yesterday
> yesterday afternoon

a It is September 19th now. In August, Martha went to the opera.
Martha went to the opera *last month.*

b On Sunday, you went swimming. Today is Tuesday.
I went swimming ....

c It is February now. From April to December, Jay worked in a factory.
Jay worked in a factory ....

d You went to bed at 12.30. It is now 9 o'clock in the morning.
I stayed up until after midnight ....

e On Saturday and Sunday, you visited a country park. Today is Friday.
We visited a wonderful country park ....

f Sasha came round for tea at 5 o'clock on Monday. It is now Tuesday.
Sasha had tea with me ....

2 *ABOUT* YOU

Write true sentences about what you did. Use sentence beginnings from Box A and endings from Box B.

A	B
I started ...	yesterday
I went ...	last week
I watched ...	yesterday afternoon
I decided ...	last year
I bought ...	the day before yesterday
I won ...	last month
I stayed ...	yesterday morning
	last summer

a *I started this unit yesterday afternoon.*

b ....

c ....

d ....

e ....

f ....

g ....

More practice

Past Simple + **ago**

a long time ago

a few months ago

four years ago

one week ago

two days ago

DOWNLOADS: 50,000

I bought my first guitar a long time ago. We started our band *ThunderMusic* four years ago. We had a big hit a few months ago. 50,000 people bought our song! One week ago we won Best Song of the Year. We argued! The band broke up two days ago!

We use *ago* to say how long before now something happened. We are looking backwards into the past.

They went on holiday two months ago.

July   August   September   October (now)

If someone asks you 'When did it happen?' you could say (1) a time or date or (2) use *ago*.

When did you meet your boyfriend?

In January.

Six months ago.

1 Read the information. Then make sentences with *ago*.

a Tom bought a new watch on Tuesday. Today is Friday.
Tom bought a new watch three days ago.

b The train left at 12.20. The time now is 12.25.

c Sharon passed her exam in 2012.

d Patrick phoned Dexter at 8.00. It is now 9.30.

e I moved to Denver in January. It's October now.

f Sheila first heard this song on 7 March. It's now 21 March.

g Shakespeare died in 1616.

h My uncle gave me this toy car when I was a baby. I am now 83!

2 ABOUT YOU

Write true sentences about yourself. Use *ago*.

a I was born

b I had my first English lesson

c My most recent English lesson was

d My birthday was

e I woke up

f I started work on this unit

g I first tasted coffee

h I used a computer for the first time

More practice

I can ... Describe a journey

Past Simple + prepositions of movement

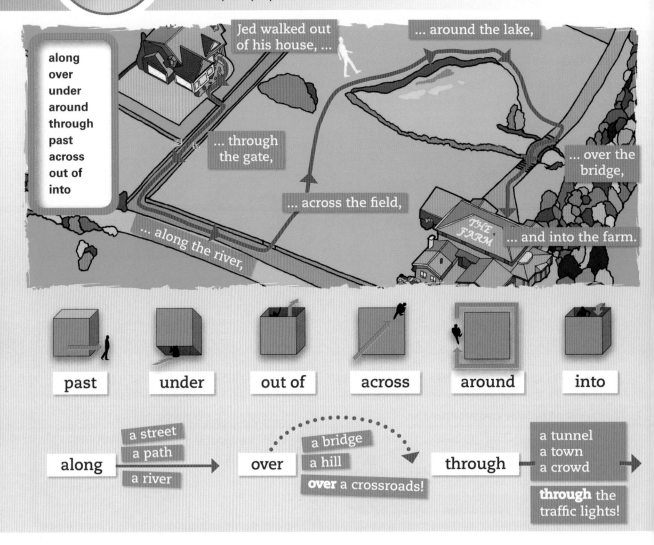

along
over
under
around
through
past
across
out of
into

Jed walked out of his house, ...

... around the lake,

... through the gate,

... over the bridge,

... across the field,

THE FARM

... and into the farm.

... along the river,

past | under | out of | across | around | into

along → a street / a path / a river

over → a bridge / a hill | **over** a crossroads!

through → a tunnel / a town / a crowd | **through** the traffic lights!

---

1 Look at the picture of the Old Town. Match sentences a–f with 1–6.

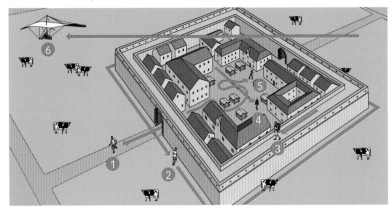

a Jessie walked along the old town wall. ......**3**......

b Bill flew over the town in his hang-glider. ....

c Piotr ran out of the town. ....

d Sandra skated through the Old Town. ....

e Wlodek jogged around the town. ....

f Angus walked across the town square. ....

2 <u>Underline</u> the correct word.

a The children ran <u>*out of*</u> / *over* school at the end of their lessons.

b We walked *into* / *across* the tunnel. It was really dark inside.

c Charlie ran *through* / *over* the crowd and finished the marathon.

d Last night at the circus I saw a six-year-old boy walk *into* / *along* a rope 20 metres above ground!

e We walked all *around* / *through* the strange building, but we couldn't find a door to go inside.

f Our plane flew *around* / *over* the Alps and landed in Zurich.

g Chas walked *along* / *over* the river for ten miles before he found a small village.

More practice

She ran past the window. **I waved at her.**

We went to the buffet. **We talked about astronomy.**

She ran past the window and I waved at her.

We went to the buffet and talked about astronomy.

> We don't need to repeat the subject (e.g. 'we') if it's the same.

I went to the opera last night. **I left after 30 minutes.**

I went to the opera last night, but left after 30 minutes.

> After 'but' there is something contrasting, surprising or negative.

---

1 Join the two sentences with *and*. Don't repeat the pronoun if it isn't needed.

a Bianca sat down. She started reading her magazine.
Bianca sat down and started reading her magazine.

b I went to the petrol station. I bought some flowers.

c Carrie turned the TV on. She watched the news.

d Dan came to the meeting late. He yawned all the time.

e Monty rang the doorbell. Lara opened the door.

f I arrived at 9.00. I went straight to Reception.

2 Join the two sentences with *but*. Don't repeat the pronoun if it isn't needed.

a It was a lovely day. I was ill in bed.
It was a lovely day, but I was ill in bed.

b Tony phoned his girlfriend three times. No one answered.

c Eva won the race. She didn't win a medal.

d Maria ate a lot of paella. She didn't have dessert.

e The music was wonderful. It was too loud.

f I failed my exam. It doesn't matter.

3 Join the two sentences with *and* or *but*.

a It was a lovely day. We had a great picnic.
It was a lovely day and we had a great picnic.

b We decided to have a picnic. It started to rain.
We decided to have a picnic, but it started to rain.

c I went to the hairdresser's yesterday. They didn't have any space for me.

d I went to the hairdresser's yesterday. I had a great cut.

e We apologised for our noisy party. We gave them some flowers.

f We apologised for our noisy party. They were still angry.

g We were lost in the desert near Riyadh. We didn't have much water.

h We were lost in the desert. We had a lot of water.

More practice

Talk about reasons and results

Past Simple + **so/because**

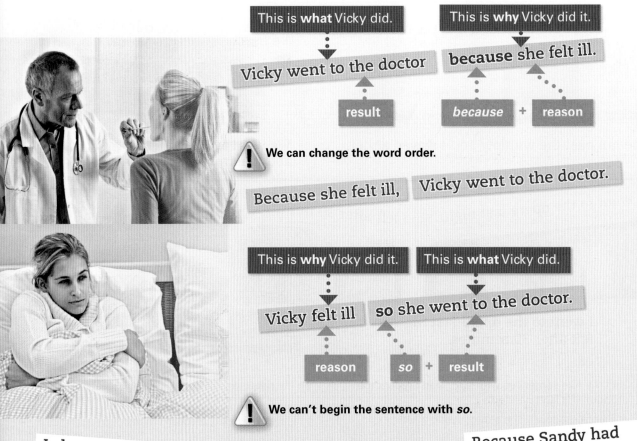

This is **what** Vicky did.

Vicky went to the doctor

result

This is **why** Vicky did it.

because she felt ill.

because + **reason**

⚠ **We can change the word order.**

Because she felt ill, Vicky went to the doctor.

This is **why** Vicky did it.

This is **what** Vicky did.

Vicky felt ill **so** she went to the doctor.

reason so + **result**

⚠ **We can't begin the sentence with *so*.**

I cleaned the car because it was really dirty.

It was late so I went home.

I was worried so I called you.

Because Sandy had low marks, we spoke to her teacher.

1 Complete the sentences with *because* or *so*.

a The children went to bed __because__ they were very tired.

b I bought his new book _____ I wanted to read it.

c The plane's engine had a problem _____ we all got off.

d The clouds were dark _____ I took my umbrella.

e _____ there was a lot of snow, the school closed.

f We went to The Stream Café _____ everyone told us it was fantastic.

g Fatima had a problem with her teeth _____ she went to the dentist.

h I was bored _____ I decided to phone you!

2 Read the situations. Then write sentences with *so* or *because*.

a Mike wanted to buy new headphones. The shop was closed.
Mike didn't buy new headphones *because the shop was closed.*

b Mike wanted to phone Cindy, but it was very late. He didn't phone her.
It was very late _____

c Mike didn't go to work. He didn't feel very well.
Mike didn't feel very well _____

d Yesterday Mike told Cindy that Mahler's 2nd Symphony was wonderful. Cindy listened to it today.
Mike recommended Mahler's 2nd Symphony _____

e Mike saw some beautiful blue earrings in a shop. He liked them. He bought them for Cindy.
Mike bought some beautiful blue earrings for Cindy _____

f Mike wanted to catch the bus. The bus arrived at the stop. It was full. He didn't get on.
The bus was full _____

More practice

Past Simple • narrative

Say when it happened

Introduce the story. Say what it is about in a short way.

Use Past Simple verbs to tell the main story: *started; skied; put up; slept; arrived; jumped; put,* etc.

Introduce negative events with *unfortunately.* We can introduce positive events with *fortunately.*

Use *was / were* to describe the weather, the temperature, etc.

Use time words to help put the story in order: *first, then, before, after, finally,* etc.

Say when actions happened: *Every night, one night,* etc.

End the story. You can summarise, say how you feel, talk about the future, etc.

... and how you felt

Last year I walked to the South Pole! Yes, really! We started at the end of December. We skied 800 kilometres. The temperature was sometimes - 45°. Every night we put up tents and slept in them. There were lots of storms. Unfortunately, one night a tent blew away! Finally, on the 20th January we arrived at the South Pole. I was so happy. I jumped up and down then put my flag in the ground. It took 24 days. I am very glad I did it – but I never want to do it again!

1 Complete the story using the verbs in brackets in the Past Simple.

I ..... *went* ..... ª (go) to visit a friend who lives on the other side of town. I .... ᵇ (catch) the tram from my flat to the centre. It .... ᶜ (break) down after just one stop! I .... ᵈ (get) off and .... ᵉ (walk)! In the town centre, I .... ᶠ (get) on the metro. It .... ᵍ (not move)! We .... ʰ (sit) on the train for 40 minutes. They .... ⁱ (announce) that the next station was closed. The doors .... ʲ (open). I .... ᵏ (run) back up to the street and .... ˡ (take) a taxi. Just 30 seconds before we .... ᵐ (arrive) I .... ⁿ (realise) that I .... ᵒ (not have) any money! I .... ᵖ (knock) on my friend's front door to borrow €10. And do you know what? He wasn't in! It really wasn't a great day for me!

2 Look again at **1.** Where could you add these words to the story? (You can join sentences and change the punctuation. Different answers may be possible.)

a Last week
Last week I went to visit a friend ...

b First
....

c Unfortunately
....

d Then
....

3 ***ABOUT* YOU**

Write a short story about something you did last year. Use five verbs from the box.

arrived bought came caught felt
heard met saw started stopped
tried was/were went

Last year I ...

I can ...
Use the Past Simple

Past Simple review

1 Write questions to ask your friend.

a where she went at the weekend
Where did you go at the weekend?

b if she caught the last bus
Did you catch the last bus?

c what she ate for lunch

d why she went on a diet

e what she bought at the shops

f how much her new mobile phone cost

g if she sang at the party

h when she got home last night

i if she told her parents about the show

j why she phoned you

2 Paddy has a nine-month-old baby boy, Oliver.
Tonight Polly, the mum, is at a meeting and Paddy
has to look after Oliver. At 9 p.m. Polly phones
Paddy and checks how things are. Put the verbs
in brackets in the correct past form (positive,
negative or question).

Polly: *Did you give* ᵃ
(you / give) Oliver
a bath?

Paddy: Yes, I did.

Polly: _____ ᵇ
(you / check) the
water? It wasn't
too hot?

Paddy: _____ ᶜ
(I / check) it. It was
fine.

Polly: _____ ᵈ (he / like) his bath?

Paddy: No, _____ ᵉ (he / cry) all the time.
_____ ᶠ (he / enjoy) it!

Polly: Oh dear! What _____ ᵍ (you / do)?

Paddy: _____ ʰ (I / sing) songs to him for
an hour!

Polly: What about food? _____ ⁱ (you /
give) him some milk?

Paddy: Oh! How stupid! _____ ʲ (I / forget)!
_____ ᵏ (I / give) him any milk!

3 Complete the story with the verbs in brackets in the
correct form. They might be positive or negative.

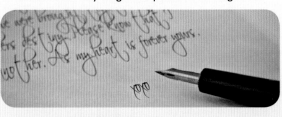

a When Steve was young he ___studied___ calligraphy
– the art of writing beautiful letters. (study)

b Unfortunately, he _didn't enjoy_ it. (enjoy)

c He always _____ bored in class. (feel)

d Every day his teacher _____ him, (tell)

e 'You _____ this well. It isn't good enough.' (do)

f Many years later Steve _____ to university. (go)

g He was still quite lazy and he _____ very hard
on his course. (work)

h But he _____ to write computer programs ...
(learn)

i and _____ a beautiful calendar app. (design)

j It _____ many beautiful letters. (use)

k He _____ it was anything special ... (think)

l but lots of people _____ it ... (buy)

m and he _____ very rich! (become)

n 'How strange!' he _____ (say)

o 'When I was young I _____ calligraphy.' (like)

4 Read the conversations. Write the questions. Use
the verbs in brackets

a Paul: Do you like my new hat?
Sue: *Where did you get it?* (get)?
Paul: At a small shop near the station.

b Sharon: I went to the emergency dentist
yesterday evening.
Sam: _____ (go)?
Sharon: Because I had a terrible toothache.

c Van: Wow! That was a very expensive meal!
Ted: _____ (cost)?
Van: More than £40!

d Pete: She asked me if I liked her hair! I didn't
want to be rude!
Tom: _____ (say)?
Pete: I said it was 'very unusual'!

e Wilma: I'm so sorry I missed your party!
Linda: _____ (forget)?
Wilma: Yes, I did. I didn't write it in my diary.

f Shah: Right. Here's supper! Help yourself!
Lucy: _____ (cook)?
Shah: Yes! All by myself!

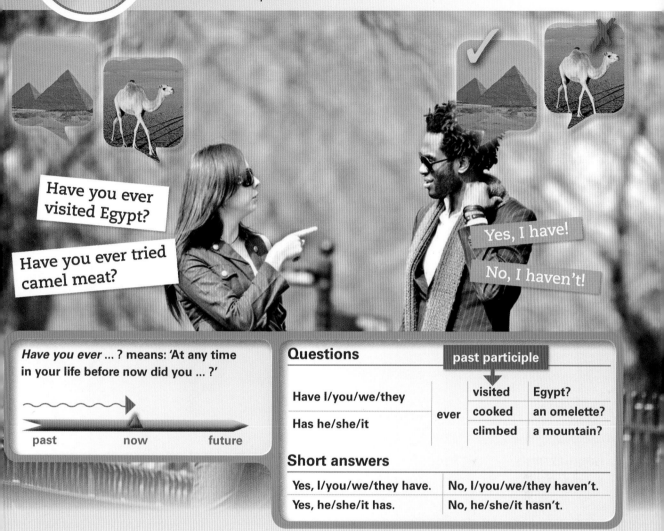

Have you ever visited Egypt?

Have you ever tried camel meat?

Yes, I have!

No, I haven't!

Have you ever ... ? means: 'At any time in your life before now did you ... ?'

past   now   future

Questions

			past participle	
Have I/you/we/they		**ever**	**visited**	**Egypt?**
Has he/she/it			**cooked**	**an omelette?**
			climbed	**a mountain?**

Short answers

Yes, I/you/we/they have.	No, I/you/we/they haven't.
Yes, he/she/it has.	No, he/she/it hasn't.

---

1 Make questions to ask a friend.

a watch / TV all night?
Have you ever watched TV all night?

b paint / a house?

c dance / on a beach at night?

d cook / Indian food?

e play / *Final Fantasy*?

f call / the wrong phone number?

g talk / for more than an hour on the phone?

h walk / to work or school?

2 ABOUT YOU

Give true answers to the questions about your life.

a Have you ever walked on the moon?
No, I haven't.

b Have you ever played basketball?

c Have you ever talked to a film star?

d Have you ever had a full English breakfast?

e Have you ever owned a pet?

f Have you ever lived in your country's capital city?

g Have you ever cried during a sad film?

h Have you ever played table tennis?

More practice

Past participles • Present Perfect **Have you ever** ... questions

> We need past participles to make Present Perfect questions and sentences.

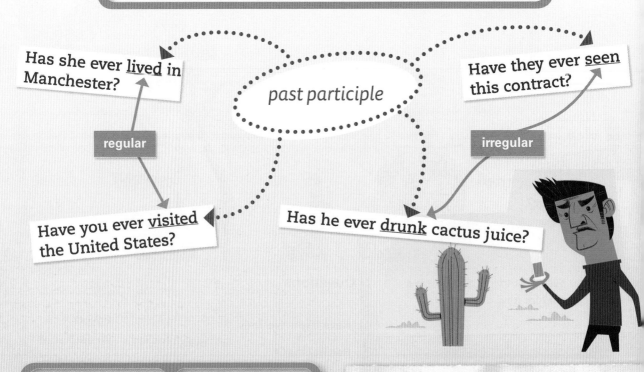

Has she ever <u>lived</u> in Manchester?

Have they ever <u>seen</u> this contract?

past participle

regular

irregular

Have you ever <u>visited</u> the United States?

Has he ever <u>drunk</u> cactus juice?

Regular verb + -ed/d

live → lived

visit → visited

wash → washed

Irregular verbs are different.

drink → drunk

see → seen

write → written

There is a list of irregular verbs on page 127. Don't confuse the Past Simple and the past participle!

	Column 2: Past Simple	Column 3: past participle
buy	bought	bought
drive	drove	driven
forget	forgot	forgotten
go	went	gone
...	...	...

Past participles may be the same as Past Simple – or they could be different!

---

1 Match the verbs and noun phrases to make questions.

Have you ever

a	grown	1	chickens?
b	sung	2	vegetables?
c	ridden	3	a cold?
d	caught	4	a lie?
e	told	5	a motorbike?
f	kept	6	opera?

2 Only two of the verbs in the box add *-ed* to make a past participle. Which two? (Check on page 127.)

> be climb collect drive eat
> fly hear lose run swim

....
....

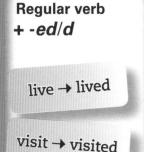

3 Use the verbs from the list in **2** to complete the questions. Put them in the correct past participle form.

a Have you ever ___been___ in the Antarctic?
Yes! It was beautiful.

b Have you ever _____ a Ferrari?
Yes, I have. It was so fast!

c Have you ever _____ a lion roar?
No, I haven't. Is it very loud?

d Have you ever _____ sushi?
Yes! Many times! I love it!

e Have you ever _____ a mountain?
No. I'm frightened of high places!

f Have you ever _____ a marathon?
No. I'm very bad at athletics!

g Have you ever _____ with dolphins?
Yes, I have. It was amazing!

h Have you ever _____ in a hang-glider?
No, I haven't.

i Have you ever _____ stamps?
No. I think it's a bit boring!

j Have you ever _____ your suitcase?
Yes – twice!

4 Use the verb list (page 127) to find the Past Simple (2) and past participles (3) of these verbs.

1	2	3
begin	*began*	*begun*
become		
blow		
begin		
catch		
come		
choose		
draw		
feel		
find		
freeze		
give		
know		
leave		
make		
say		
speak		
take		
win		
write		

5 Make questions to ask a friend.

a eat / Korean food?
Have you ever eaten Korean food?

b sing / in a karaoke bar

c leave / a film before the end

d forget / someone's birthday

e break / your leg

f ride / a horse

g see / a ghost

h go / on holiday on your own

6 **ABOUT** **YOU**

Complete the questions using the verbs in brackets. Then give true answers about your life.

a Have you ever ___visited___ the Antarctic? (visit)
No, I haven't.

b Have you ever _____ a famous person? (meet)

c Have you ever _____ a full English breakfast? (have)

d Have you ever _____ a penguin? (see)

e Have you ever _____ a big prize? (win)

f Have you ever _____ a truck? (drive)

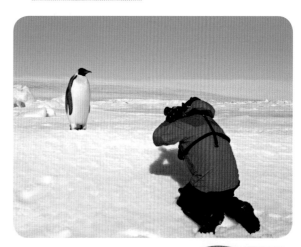

Present Perfect + **never**

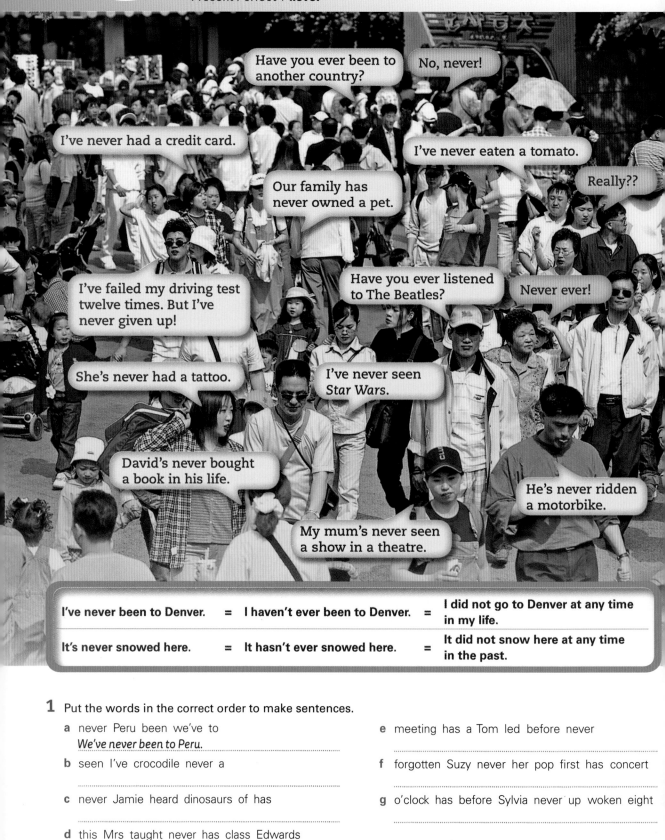

| I've never been to Denver. | = | I haven't ever been to Denver. | = | I did not go to Denver at any time in my life. |
| It's never snowed here. | = | It hasn't ever snowed here. | = | It did not snow here at any time in the past. |

1 Put the words in the correct order to make sentences.

a never Peru been we've to
We've never been to Peru.

b seen I've crocodile never a

c never Jamie heard dinosaurs of has

d this Mrs taught never has class Edwards

e meeting has a Tom led before never

f forgotten Suzy never her pop first has concert

g o'clock has before Sylvia never up woken eight

2 Tell your friend about ...

a a film you've never seen.
I've never seen Star Wars.

b a book you've never read.

c a place you have never been to.

d a food you have never eaten.

e a sport or game you have never played.

f a singer you've never listened to.

g something you have never done.

3 *ABOUT* **YOU**

Look at these interesting things to do. Make some true 'never' sentences about you, your family and friends.

meet an astronaut

climb a mountain

see an eclipse of the Sun

be a model in a fashion show

write a detective story

eat a snake

sail around the world

visit the Great Wall of China

a I *'ve never met an astronaut.*
b I
c My teacher
d My parents
e My best friend
f Students in our class

4 Complete the sentences (different answers may be possible). <u>Keep the same verb.</u>

a Harry has played tennis many times, but he *'s never played volleyball.*

b Eva has cooked lots of different meals, but she *'s never cooked a curry.*

c Meena has swum in the Atlantic Ocean, but she

d Tom has owned lots of cars, but he

e Joanna has worked in five different countries, but she

f I've listened to lots of pop music, but I

5 *THE* **TOUGH** *ONE*

Complete the sentences. Use a different verb!

a Harry has played tennis many times, but he *'s never beaten me!*

b Eva has cooked lots of different meals, but he *'s never baked a cake.*

c Meena has swum in the Atlantic Ocean, but she

d Tom has owned lots of cars, but he

e Joanna has worked in five different countries, but she

f I've listened to lots of pop music, but I

6 *ABOUT* **YOU**

Write some true sentences about yourself, using your own ideas.

a I
b I
c I
d I

I can ... Talk about experiences and events 'before now'

Present Perfect tense • up to now

I've travelled all around the country by train.

You've never told me the truth!

He's never been to a library.

We've been here before.

She's never seen a kangaroo!

I've heard about this program.

He's worked in seven different restaurant kitchens.

He's never understood this.

You've written three books! Wow!

She's been to Bangkok.

It's never worked.

We've tried everything.

They've come to our house lots of times.

| I/You/We/They | + 've/have | + past participle |
| He/She/It | + 's/has | |

The **Present Perfect** tells us about experiences or things that happened (or never happened) at some time *before now*. The tense does not tell us exactly when things happened.

past   now   future

1 Put the words in the correct order.

a always Austria he's in lived
   He's always lived in Austria.

b on I've train been a never
   ....

c loved cream she's ice always
   ....

d times zoo we've to many the been
   ....

e I've Kenya never to been
   ....

2 Write sentences about things Alia has done.

a go / Australia
   She's been to Australia.

b read / all the Harry Potter books
   ....

c start / her own website
   ....

d design / beautiful baby clothes
   ....

e make / lots of money
   ....

f write / many magazine articles
   ....

3 **ABOUT** YOU

Use the word pool to write five sentences about you and people you know.

I   has   in   flown   here

My father   have   to   lived   a kangaroo

My best friends   Asia   on   been   a ship

My teacher   Europe   never   seen   a helicopter

America   always   worked   a UFO

....
....
....
....
....

More practice

Present Perfect for completed actions

The actions were in the PAST ... but ... we can see the RESULT now.

I've worked all day! Look! !Ta daaaaaaahh!

I've tidied the toys.

I've put the books back on the shelf.

She's cleaned the windows.

She's mended the chair.

9 a.m.

I've vacuumed the carpet.

I've washed the curtains.

7 p.m.

She's done everything!

1 Tell your friend what you have done.

a tidy / room   *I've tidied the room.*
b clean / the bathroom ....
c wash / the clothes ....
d buy / some fresh vegetables ....
e make / the supper ....

f phone / Kolya ....
g tell / him the news ....
h pay / the electricity bill ....
i mend / the hole in the wall ....

2 Write the sentences. Use the verbs in the box in the Present Perfect.

cut ~~finish~~ make mend open paint

	Past	Now
a		

Sarah

Sarah's finished the jigsaw.

b

Tom

c

Brian

cupboard

	Past	Now
d	grass	

Molly

e tap

Jack

f

Eva

I can ...

Talk about past actions that have a result now

Present Perfect for past actions with a connection to now

What's wrong?

action in past

result NOW

I've broken my pen!

(... and now I can't write the test!)

I've brought the wrong passport!

(... and now I can't get on the plane)

My exam results email hasn't arrived!

(... and now I don't know if I passed!)

Mum's lost her wallet!

(... and now she's very worried)

The train has left!

(... and now we'll be very late for the show)

It's started raining.

(... and now we can't go out)

> **The action was in the past ... but we see or feel the result now.**

1 Tell your friend what has happened.

a the film / start
The film has started.

b l / break / my arm
....

c our teacher / lose / her laptop
....

d a bear / steal / our honey
....

e they / arrive
....

f you / do / it again!
....

c

Jen

d

2 Write the sentences. Use the verbs in the box.

> buy   cut   ~~drop~~   land   leave   stop

Past	Now

a Steve

Steve's dropped the paint.

b

e

PAY HERE   Mark

f

More practice

Present perfect + **just**

She's **just** heard the news!

The President's **just** arrived!

Have you **just** bought that?

I've **just** passed my test!

They've **just** won!

just means 'very close to now' – perhaps only a few minutes ago.

1 Look at the pictures. What has just happened?

break ~~drop~~ eat fall score win

a

He's just dropped his cup of coffee.

b

.... the race.

c

....
....

d

.... down the ladder.

e

.... a goal.

f

....
....

2 Bess, Brad and their children are getting ready for a dinner party. Bess asks Brad what people have just done. Write his sentences.

a I / laid / the table
   I've just laid the table.
b Grace / tidy / her room
   ....
c Josh / turn on / the music
   ....
d the baby / fall asleep
   ....
e our computer / crash
   ....
f the guests / arrive
   ....

3 **ABOUT** YOU
Write three things that you and other people have just done.

a I've just ....
b .... has just ....
c .... have just ....

I can ... **Choose *gone* or *been***

Past participles of **go**

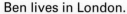
Ben lives in London.

London

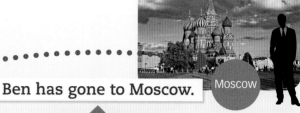
Moscow

Ben has gone to Moscow.

(= he is there)

London

Moscow

Ben has been to Moscow.

(= he is back in London)

1 Omar and Judy are chatting in the office. Complete the sentences with *been* or *gone*.

Judy Mike! Nice to see you! Where have you ___*been*___ ᵃ?

Omar Oh – I've _____ ᵇ at home. I was ill.

Judy Oh dear! I hope you feel better.

Omar Yes, thanks. Sarah's seat is empty! Where has she _____ ᶜ?

Judy She's _____ ᵈ on a trip to Argentina.

Omar Oh, yes. I think she's _____ ᵉ there before, hasn't she?

Judy No, she's never _____ ᶠ there. But she has _____ ᵍ to Uruguay and Brazil.

Omar Has she _____ ʰ for long?

Judy No, it's only a three-day visit. Have you ever _____ ⁱ to Latin America?

Omar No, but I'd love to one day! Where's Barney?

Judy Oh – he's _____ ʲ home early today. I think he's ill now!

2 Complete the sentences with *been* or *gone*.

a Your hair looks lovely! Have you ___*been*___ to the hairdresser's?

b Has Chloe ever _____ to Africa?

c Sorry, you can't speak to Mr Roy. He's _____ out to lunch.

d Fiona can tell you all about Disneyland. She's _____ seven times!

e You'll have to phone again tomorrow. I'm afraid the manager has _____ home.

f There's a new art gallery in King Street. Have you _____ to it?

g Goodness! Where has my shopping list _____? I can't find it.

h How nice to see you again! Where have you _____ this week?

More practice

Present Perfect negatives + **yet**

Do you like that new app?

I haven't tried it yet.

Is that a good book?

It's OK – but I haven't finished it yet.

What's for supper?

I don't know. I haven't made it yet. In fact, I haven't started ... Sorry!

yet in a negative sentence = not until now
(... but I think it probably will happen or be true in the future)

I/You/We/They	haven't	made	a decision	(yet).
		tidied	the room	
He/She/It	hasn't	seen	him	
		bought	a present	

1 Match the sentence halves.

a I want to go out for a walk,
b I need to ask my boss a question,
c I want to buy a train ticket,
d I'd like to call my new girlfriend,
e I want to play on my computer,
f New York is an amazing city,

1 but I haven't mended it yet.
2 but it hasn't stopped raining yet.
3 but she hasn't told me her number yet.
4 but his meeting hasn't finished yet.
5 but I haven't been there yet.
6 but the station hasn't opened yet.

2 Read Wendy's questions and give 'I don't know' negative answers using the verbs in brackets.

a Do you like the DVD? (watch)
I don't know. I haven't watched it yet.

b Who sent you that letter? (open)

c Is the soup tasty? (try)

d What did John think about the news? (tell)

e Is the new shopping mall interesting? (go)

f Are your new neighbours friendly? (meet)

g Is the homework difficult? (do)

h Is that the correct number for George? (ring)

3 Complete the sentences with *just* or *yet*. (Look at Unit 61 if you need to revise *just*.)

a Sorry! I've ..... *just* ..... broken your pencil.
b You're in time. The train hasn't left ....
c I don't know if I like her new CD. I haven't listened to it ....
d I've .... heard the news about Argentina!
e Susie has bought the book, but she hasn't read it ....
f I'm very tired. I've .... finished my work.
g 'Have you seen that new film with Jennifer Lawrence?'
   'Not ....?'
h 'Have you finished Exercise 3?'
   '............... !'

Present Perfect + **already**

Roger expected the ferry to leave at 11 o'clock. It's 10.50 now.

The ferry has already left.

(= It left **before now** & it left **before I expected**.)

It's already left!

| I **expected** it to leave **in the future**. | ... but it left **before now** – in the past | ... and I'm surprised! |

past   now   future

The guests have already arrived!
(= The guests came before now. I expected them to come later.)

Sorry, John! The meeting has already finished.
(= The meeting finished before now. John expected it to finish later.)

'Are you going to read that story tonight?'
'I've already read it.'
(= I read the book before now. You expected me to read it later.)

1 Put the words in the correct order.

a exhibition seen already I've the
  I've already seen the exhibition.

b been shops already to she's the
  ....

c the already started has race
  ....

d paid tickets I've for already the
  ....

e snow started has to it already ?
  ....

2 Answer with *already*.

a When will the meeting finish?
  It has already finished.

b Please phone your mother.
  I've already phoned her.

c When will the plane land?
  It ....

d Tell your sister that lunch is ready.
  I .... her.

e When will the lesson start?
  It ....

f Would you like to see this film?
  I .... it.

3 THE **TOUGH** ONE
Give answers with *already*. Think about possible verbs!

a Let's go to the new museum!
  I ....

b I want the last piece of cake.
  Sorry! I ....

c Happy birthday! I think you'll enjoy this book!
  Oh dear! I ....

More practice

Present Perfect + **for** and **since**

How long have you worked here?

Since 1st January.

For four months.

since – only with present perfect

for – with present perfect AND past simple e.g. *She's worked here since February. He worked in Sweden for 25 years.*

since = the start

January February March April May June July August

past | **for** = how long it was → now | future

---

1 Complete the phrases with *for* or *since*.

a	..*for*.. twenty minutes	**f**	.... seven years
b	.... 9 o'clock	**g**	.... last week
c	.... a week	**h**	.... two days
d	.... September	**i**	.... last night
e	 2011	**j**	.... three hours

2 ABOUT YOU

Give true answers.

a How long have you been at school?
Since ....

b How long have you been an English student?
For ....

c How long have you lived at the place where you live now?
Since ....

d What's your favourite sport?
....
How long have you done it?
For ....

e How long have you been in this room?
Since ....

3 Complete the sentences.

a I arrived at 2 p.m. I've been here for two hours. The time now is ...*4 p.m.*..

b We came to the restaurant at 8.30 p.m. We've been here for two and a half hours. The time now is ....

c It's midday. Ellie's been at work for two hours. She's been here since ....

d We've lived here since 1 January last year. It's now 1 January again. We've lived here for ....

e We arrived at the hotel on Monday night. We left on Wednesday morning. We stayed for ....

f It's Sunday morning now. We're leaving the camp. We stayed here for three nights. We've been here since ....

 **I can ...**

Choose whether to use Past Simple or Present Perfect

Comparison of Past Simple and Present Perfect

She won first prize!

Past Simple

An event that happened in the past that has **no direct connection to now**.

It feels like something that **started** and **finished** in the past.

Past Simple

We are thinking about a **specific time in the past**: a moment, a time, a date or period when something happened.

She's won first prize!

Present Perfect

An event in the past that **has some connection to now**.

It feels **live** and important **now**. It is still **news**.

Present Perfect

We are not interested in **when** something happened. We are more interested in the memory or experience that we have **now**.

Make a quick decision

Time reference

If there is a time reference to a finished past time (e.g. *yesterday, last night, at two o'clock, in January, when you were young,* etc.), then you need the **Past Simple**, not the Present Perfect!

when

If you ask a question with *when*, use the **Past Simple**.

Sometimes, both tenses are possible.

Choose the **Present Perfect** if you want something to sound like news.

• *The President resigned!*

This one sounds like **history**.

• *The President's resigned!*

This one sounds like **news**.

News programmes often use the Present Perfect so that stories will sound up-to-date.

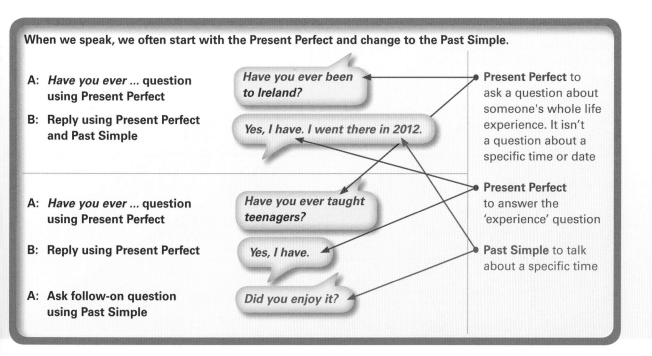

When we speak, we often start with the Present Perfect and change to the Past Simple.

A: *Have you ever ...* question using Present Perfect

Have you ever been to Ireland?

B: Reply using Present Perfect and Past Simple

Yes, I have. I went there in 2012.

Present Perfect to ask a question about someone's whole life experience. It isn't a question about a specific time or date

A: *Have you ever ...* question using Present Perfect

Have you ever taught teenagers?

B: Reply using Present Perfect

Yes, I have.

Present Perfect to answer the 'experience' question

A: Ask follow-on question using Past Simple

Did you enjoy it?

Past Simple to talk about a specific time

---

1 Underline the correct tense.

a You've been to Vietnam! How interesting. <u>*When did you go?*</u> / *When have you been?*

b Shakespeare *lived* / *has lived* from 1564 to 1616.

c I *just found* / *'ve just found* my wallet.

d *Did you ever try* / *Have you ever tried* riding a skateboard?

e I *worked* / *have worked* in China until 2011.

f Listen to the news! The Minister for Education *resigned* / *has resigned*!

g I *went* / *have been* to college in 2012.

h *Did you have* / *Have you had* a bike when you were a child?

2 Complete the sentences using the Present Perfect or the Past Simple and the verbs in brackets.

a Tom bought the house in January 1995. He sold it in December 2000.
He ___owned___ (own) the house for five years.

b Shari is a manager for Trax. She started in 2002.
She _____ (work) for Trax for many years.

c Tariq was a manager with Trax. He resigned in 2009.
He _____ (work) for Trax for many years.

d María is on holiday. She arrived in India on Sunday.
María _____ (be) in India since Sunday.

e María had a two week holiday in India. She came back home to Madrid last night.
María _____ (be) in India for two weeks.

3 Write possible questions for the answers. (Different questions may be possible.)

a How long _have you lived in this town?_ (live)?
Since 2010

b When _____ (go)?
In January.

c Have you _____ (do)?
No. I've never done that.

d Why _____ (go)?
Because I wanted to learn German.

e What _____ (buy)?
He bought a new camera.

f Where _____ (go)?
I think he's gone to the bank.

4 **ABOUT** YOU
Write some similar questions to ask yourself. Then ... answer them!

a How long _____

b When _____

c Have you _____

d Why _____

e What _____

Past Progressive

Michael started playing *Crime City* at 10 a.m.
He stopped playing at 8 p.m.

His friend Jeff phones him at 11 p.m.

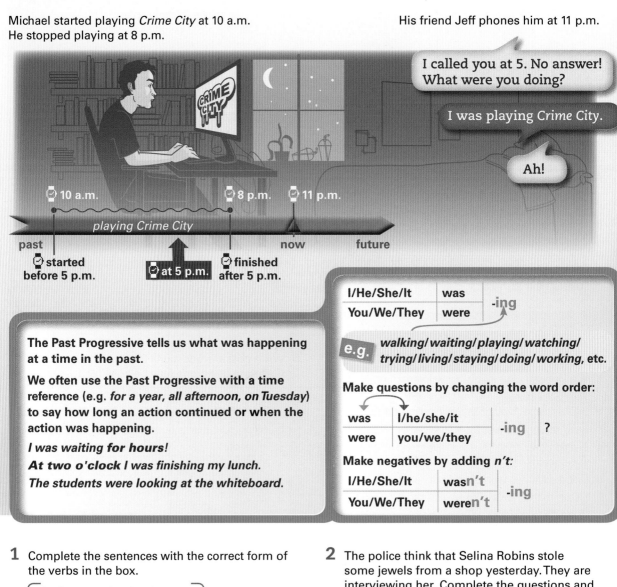

I called you at 5. No answer! What were you doing?

I was playing *Crime City*.

Ah!

The Past Progressive tells us what was happening at a time in the past.

We often use the Past Progressive with a time reference (e.g. *for a year, all afternoon, on Tuesday*) to say how long an action continued or when the action was happening.

I was waiting for hours!
At two o'clock I was finishing my lunch.
The students were looking at the whiteboard.

| I/He/She/It | was | -ing |
| You/We/They | were | |

e.g. *walking/ waiting/ playing/ watching/ trying/ living/ staying/ doing/ working*, etc.

Make questions by changing the word order:

| was | I/he/she/it | -ing | ? |
| were | you/we/they | | |

Make negatives by adding *n't*:

| I/He/She/It | wasn't | -ing |
| You/We/They | weren't | |

1 Complete the sentences with the correct form of the verbs in the box.

> bark cry ~~do~~ laugh not look rain study text

a What __were__ you __doing__ last night?
b We didn't go to the outdoor swimming pool because it _____ .
c I'm so tired! The baby _____ all night!
d That horrible dog _____ at midnight!
e When you looked in her room, _____ Sarah _____ for her exams?
f They _____ ! That's why they bumped into each other!
g I _____ you all evening– but you never saw my messages! Why didn't you check your phone?
h It was a really funny show! I _____ for two hours!

2 The police think that Selina Robins stole some jewels from a shop yesterday. They are interviewing her. Complete the questions and sentences using the verbs in brackets.

Police: What __were__ you __doing__ a (you/do) at 3 o'clock yesterday afternoon?
Selina: _____ b (I/watch) a film at the cinema.
Police: What film _____ c (you/watch)?
Selina: I can't remember. A horror film.
Police: Where _____ d (you/sit)?
Selina: At the front.
Police: Well. We think that at 3 o'clock _____ e (you/drive) to Westford, and at four _____ f (you/look) at jewels in Scott's jewellers.
Selina: Rubbish! At that time _____ g (I/have) a coffee with my friends.

 More practice

Interrupted Past Progressive

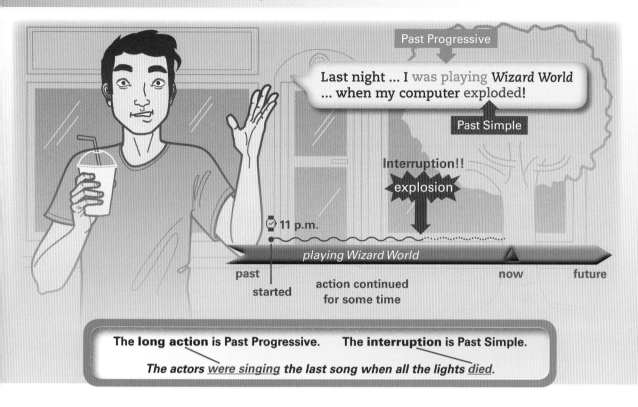

Past Progressive

Last night ... I was playing *Wizard World*
... when my computer exploded!

Past Simple

Interruption!!
explosion

11 p.m.

playing Wizard World

past | now | future
started | action continued for some time

The **long action** is Past Progressive.   The **interruption** is Past Simple.

The actors <u>were singing</u> the last song when all the lights <u>died</u>.

---

1 Say what you were doing when your friend called.

a

I was cooking dinner.

b

c

d

e

f

2 Write a sentence about each picture story.

a

Kay was doing her homework when the cat jumped on the table.

b

Sue / walk in town / fall over

c

My friends / watch TV / I / ring the bell

d

Dad / check email / fall asleep

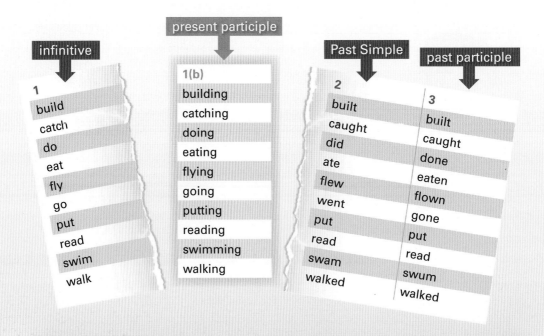

present participle

infinitive

Past Simple

past participle

1	1(b)	2	3
build	building	built	built
catch	catching	caught	caught
do	doing	did	done
eat	eating	ate	eaten
fly	flying	flew	flown
go	going	went	gone
put	putting	put	put
read	reading	read	read
swim	swimming	swam	swum
walk	walking	walked	walked

Verb lists (like the one on page 127) usually have three columns: **1** the infinitive, **2** the Past Simple form, **3** the past participle. We can easily make another column in our minds – for the present participle (the *-ing* form – **1(b)** above).

1 Answer the questions.

a Which verb form do you use to make Present Perfect sentences? *past participle, Column 3*

b Which verb form do you use to make Present Progressive sentences? ....

c Which verb form do you use to make Past Simple sentences? ....

d Which verb form do you use to make Present Simple sentences? ....

e Which verb form do you use to make Past Progressive sentences ....

f Which verb form do you use to make Past Simple questions? ....

2 In the verb list above, can you find ...

a a regular Past Simple verb? *walked*

b 4 verbs with the same spelling for Past Simple and past participle? *built, ...*

c a verb that has the same spelling and pronunciation for infinitive, Past Simple and past participle? ....

d a verb that has the same spelling for infinitive and past participle – but a different pronunciation? ....

e a verb that only changes one vowel in infinitive, Past Simple and past participle? ....

3 Complete the verb list.

1	2	3
become	became	*become* a
begin	*began* b	begun
c	bought	bought
cost	d	cost
cut	cut	e
drink	f	drunk
fall	fell	g
h	felt	felt
forget	forgot	i
j	gave	given
hide	hid	k
ride	l	ridden
run	ran	m
speak	n	o
throw	p	q
r	wore	s
write	t	u

More practice

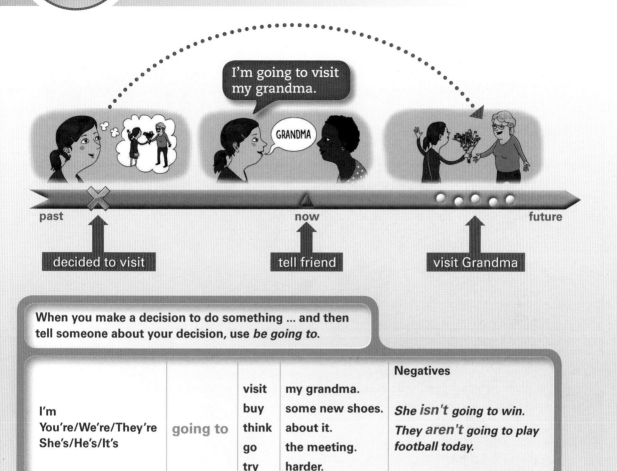

I'm going to visit my grandma.

GRANDMA

past | now | future

decided to visit | tell friend | visit Grandma

When you make a decision to do something ... and then tell someone about your decision, use *be going to*.

				Negatives
I'm You're/We're/They're She's/He's/It's	going to	visit buy think go try	my grandma. some new shoes. about it. the meeting. harder.	*She isn't going to win.* *They aren't going to play football today.*

1 What are you going to do? Match each situation a–e with two possible answers from 1–10.

a You failed an English exam.

b You burnt the supper.

c You forgot to meet your friend in town.

d You bought a new music player – but it doesn't work.

e You have to wake up very early tomorrow for an important meeting.

1 I'm going to throw it away.

2 I'm going to read the instructions again.

3 I'm going to try again next week.

4 I'm going to phone her and apologise.

5 I'm going to make some toast instead!

6 I'm going to take it back to the shop.

7 I'm going to study harder.

8 I'm going to set the alarm on my clock AND my phone.

9 I'm going to suggest a new time.

10 I'm going to go to bed early.

2 Say what you are going to do.

a

(go) *I'm going to go to the library.*

b

(go) ....
....

c

(get up) ....
....

d

(check) ....
....

e

(rescue) ....
....

f

(finish) ....
....

More practice

81

Wh- questions

What	am	I	going to	do	(about it)	?
	is	he/she/it		eat		
	are	you/we/they		say		

Where	am	I	going to	go	(...)	?
Why	is	he/she/it		stop		
When	are	you/we/they		complain		

Yes/no questions

Am	I	going to	go	(...)	?
Is	he/she/it		start		
Are	you/we/they		watch		

Short answers

Yes,	I am/she is/we are, etc.
No,	I'm not/he isn't/they aren't, etc.

1 Read the situations. Then put the words in the correct order to make questions.

a A politician is in the town centre, talking to a young family. He asks:

going vote are for you to me ?

Are you going to vote for me?

b Your friend says that she has a big problem with her washing machine. You ask:

going do about what you to it are ?

c Ken doesn't know if his friend will be at home tonight. He asks:

8 to you home are going be at at ?

d It's 7.30 in the morning. Karen feels ill. Her husband asks her:

work you today go going are to to ?

e Michael is talking to an eight-year-old boy. He asks:

going you what are be to

.... when you grow up?

f Jenna's mum sees her putting on a horrible pink skirt. She asks:

you wear are to that going really ?

2 ABOUT YOU

Write *be going to* questions to ask your friend.

a what / you / do / tonight
What are you going to do tonight?

b you / see / a film

c what / film / see

d Rick / go / too

e where / you / eat / after the film

f the children / stay / at home

g who / look after / them

More practice

We see (or hear) something **now** ... *and we predict what will happen in the* **future**

It's going to be a great party!

It's going to be fantastic!

He's going to win!

It's not going to work.

This is going to be a problem.

I'm going to cry!

past   now   future
see **now**   predict **FUTURE**

It's going to rain all night!

No ... Trust me ... It's going to stop soon!

2 What is going to happen? Write sentences using verbs from the box.

be   crash   fall   go swimming
~~land~~   rob   score   snow

a
It's going to land.

b

c

d

e

f

1 Say what you think is going to happen. Use the verbs in brackets.

a   Be careful! That dog (bite) *'s going to bite!*
b   Watch out! That shelf (fall)
c   Oh no! The steak in that pan (burn)
d   Not again! The car (break down)
e   Oh dear! Look at the baby's face. He (cry)

3 Look at the pictures. What is going to happen to your company next year? Use the verbs in the box.

> close   employ   fall   give   make
> move   ~~open~~   ~~rise~~   win

a

The company is going to open three new factories.

b

PROFITS

Profits are going to rise.

c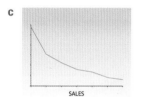

SALES

....

d

FACTORY 72

....

e

IMPORTANT NEW PRODUCT

....

f

JUST NEW PRODUCT

.... award.

g

AFRICA
HQ

....

h

$1 BILLION → CHARITY

....

i

+350

....

4 **THE TOUGH ONE**

What is going to happen? Write sentences using the verbs in the box in **2** AND some more words. Different answers may be possible.

a

....

b

....

5 Read the situations. What do the people say?

a A mother is with two young children in the theatre. The lights go out. The curtain opens. The children are still talking and making a lot of noise. The mother says,
'Sssh! *It's going to start!* '

b A man is running down the street to the station to catch a train. He hears the guard's whistle – but he is still outside the station. 'Oh no!' he says,
'I .... '

c Judy and her boyfriend, Sam, come into the room smiling. Judy holds up her hand. There is a beautiful diamond ring on her finger. Her mother says,
'Oh! You .... '

d Lots of managers are sitting round a table in the boardroom. The CEO shows a slide that says 'This year: Sales -20%'. She says,
'I'm afraid, this year, we think that sales ....
.... '

e You ate a large, fatty meal. Now you suddenly feel very ill. You say,
'Oh. I think I .... '

f Marie can't decide whether to take the PET English exam. She thinks about it all evening – then, finally, she decides: yes, she will do it! In class next day her teacher sees the completed application form and says,
'Ah. You .... '

Who did the boss tell? →	She told me. She told you. She told him. She told her. She told us. She told them.	Did you ask the security guard? Did you meet the manager? Did you eat the chocolates? Did you like the food?	→ Yes I asked him. → Yes, I met her. → Yes, I ate them! → Yes! I loved it! No! I hated it!

I →me **you** →you **he** →him **she** →her **we** →us **they** →them

Verbs often go together with a preposition. After a preposition we need an object pronoun. For example, we say *She's waiting for him* (not ✗ *for he* or ✗ *to him*).

to
*I'm **talking to you**.*
*Have you **listened to it**?*
*These books **belong to her**.*
*They **apologised to us**.*

for
*I'm **looking for it**.*
*He's **cooking** lunch **for me**.*
*She's **waiting for him**.*
*They **asked for you**.*
*She **paid for us**.*

with
*She **agreed with him**.*
Come with us!
*He **argued with her**.*

at
*She **was looking at him**.*
*We **laughed at it**.*
*I **smiled at her**.*

about
*Don't **think about it**!*
*I **worry about her**!*
*Let's **talk about me**!*

He's looking for you.

He's looking at you.

She's talking to you.

She's talking about you

1 Complete the sentences with *me, you, her, him, us* or *them*.

a This is Peter. Please tell _..him.._ what the director said.

b I couldn't hear. Please tell _____ what the director said.

c Here are Tom and Ali. Please tell _____ what he said.

d This is Sara. Please tell _____ what he said.

e We arrived late! Sorry! Please tell _____ what he said.

f You're late. Don't worry! I'll tell _____ what the director said.

2 Complete the sentences with *he/him, she/her, we/us* or *they/them*.

a I need to borrow your sync cable. Could you lend it to _..me.._?

b This is my wife's guidebook. _..She.._ bought it online.

c I've got your wife's guidebook. Please give it back to _____ . Thanks.

d That man is so rude! I really don't like _____ .

e The children are very noisy! _____ are running around and shouting.

f The children are running around and shouting. Please ask _____ to behave.

g He doesn't know which room to go to. Can you tell _____ , please?

h The boy was late for class. _____ came in at 9.35.

i I hate onions. I never eat _____ .

j I can't find my glasses! Have you seen _____ anywhere?

k _____ arrived on time but they didn't let us into the theatre.

l We asked the farmer if we could buy some butter. He gave _____ a free packet.

3 Match the beginnings and endings.

A

a When the clown fell over, the children laughed — 1 for him.
2 at him.
b The audience aren't listening 3 to him.
c Paola is cooking a meal

B

a That strange dog is looking 1 to you.
b Hector agreed 2 with you.
c That doesn't belong 3 at you.

C

a We are very late. I think Abi is waiting 1 at us.
2 with us.
b The hooligan threw a tin can 3 for us.
c John wanted you to come to the cinema

D

a Sheila is thinking hard 1 to it.
b I haven't listened 2 about it.
c We are all waiting 3 for it.

4 Complete the sentences with *to, with, for* or *about*.

a I don't want to think _..about.._ next week's exam!

b Does this bag belong _____ you?

c Quickly! Come _____ me to the Medical Room!

d After the terrible argument, our neighbours apologised _____ my wife.

e Shou and Yui are talking _____ their English class.

f Don't walk away from me! I'm talking _____ you!

g I didn't agree _____ Mr Bloomsdale.

h Mitch has lost his pet mouse. He's looked _____ it everywhere.

i I know why you're happy. I saw Harry smile _____ you!

j Don't worry! I'll pay _____ the coffees!

Apostrophe **s** • possessive pronouns

> Is this your bag?

> Is this hers?

> Yes that's mine. It's my bag.

> That's Sandra's bag.

> Whose is this?

> It's John's.

> I think this is our suitcase. It it ours?

> Is this yours?

> No, that's yours.

> I'm sorry, this isn't mine. Is it theirs?

> Is this his?

This is **my** bike.	→	It's **mine**.
This is **your** bike.	→	It's **yours**.
This is **his** bike.	→	It's **his**.
This is **her** bike.	→	It's **hers**.
This is **our** bike.	→	It's **ours**.
This is **their** bike	→	It's **theirs**.
This is **Mike's** bike.	→	It's **Mike's**.

← **mine/yours/his/ hers/ours/theirs** + noun

← **name + 's**

↑ **my/your/his/her/our/their** + noun

Use **'S** ('apostrophe s') to show that something belongs to someone

*Jack**'S** house* = the house that belongs to Jack

*the children**'S** toys*

or to show that there is a relationship or other connection

*Jack**'S** brother*

*the children**'S** drawings* = the drawings made by the children

Use **S'** ('apostrophe s') after regular plural words.

*the student**S'** work*

*our employee**S'** problems*

 *the student**'S** work* = one student
*the student**S'** work* = more than one student

Whose is this? ← = Who does this bag belong to?

Whose bag is this? ← = Is this my/your/ his/her/our/their bag?

We can use *whose* with or without a noun.

⚠

Who's your teacher? = Who is your teacher?

Who's seen the teacher? = Who has seen the teacher?

Whose teacher is that? = Is that your/his/her/ their teacher?

1 Complete the sentences with *my/mine, your/ yours, our/ours, his, her/hers* or *their/theirs*.

a 'Whose book is this?' 'Well, I gave it to you, so now it's ___yours___.'

b 'Whose book is this?' 'Well, I gave it to you, so now it's _____ book.'

c 'Is this your ring?' 'Well, I gave it to Mary so now it's _____ ring.'

d 'Whose ring is this?' 'Well, I gave it to Mary so now it's _____.'

e 'Whose scarf is this?' 'That's _____ scarf. Susie gave it to me yesterday.'

f 'Whose coat is this?' 'It's _____. Paul gave it to me yesterday.'

g 'I think this coffee pot belongs to Richard and Jane. Am I right?' 'Yes, it's _____.'

h 'I think this DVD belongs to us. Am I right?' 'Yes, it's _____.'

i 'I think this picture belongs to us. Am I right?' 'Yes, it's _____ picture.'

2 Can you complete and answer the question with six different answers?

a 'Is that ___their___ bag?'
'No. That's not ___hers___, it's ___theirs___.'

b 'Is that _____ bag?'
'No. That's not _____, it's _____.'

c 'Is that _____ bag?'
'No. That's not _____, it's _____.'

d 'Is that _____ bag?'
'No. That's not _____, it's _____.'

e 'Is that _____ bag?'
'No. That's not _____, it's _____.'

f 'Is that _____ bag?'
'No. That's not _____, it's _____.'

3 <u>Underline</u> the correct words.

a Andrew is *Damiens* / <u>*Damien's*</u> brother.

b The two *brothers* / *brother's* / *brothers'* both work for an internet company.

c They are working in the *brothers* / *brother's* / *brothers'* office.

d The photo on the desk shows the older *brothers* / *brother's* / *brothers'* wife and children.

e Damien and his wife Janet are the proud *parents* / *parent's* / *parents'* of two boys.

f Damien is the *children's* / *childrens'* father.

g The *boys* / *boy's* / *boys'* love their dad.

h The two *boys* / *boy's* / *boys'* favourite game is football.

i The youngest *boy's* / *boys* favourite food is fish fingers!

4 Complete the sentences with *who's* or *whose*.

a ___Who's___ your best friend?

b ___Whose___ phone is ringing?

c _____ got more than ten friends?

d _____ camera is this?

e _____ visited Paris?

f _____ coming to the café?

g I don't know _____ shoes these are!

h I don't know _____ leading the tour!

i _____ stories are these?

j _____ written these stories?

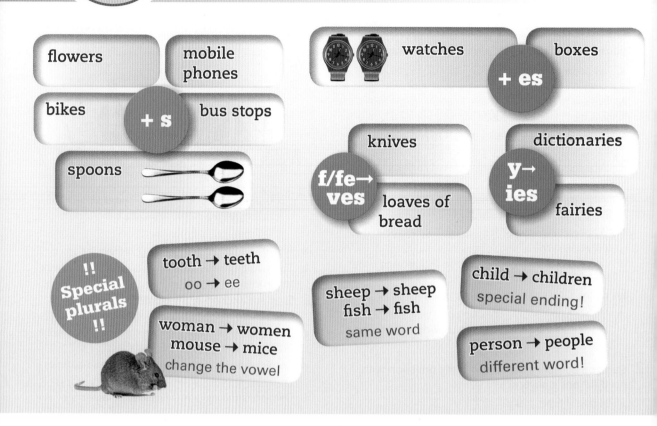

flowers

mobile phones

watches

boxes

+ es

bikes

bus stops

+ s

spoons

knives

dictionaries

f/fe→ ves

loaves of bread

y→ ies

fairies

!! Special plurals !!

tooth → teeth
oo → ee

sheep → sheep
fish → fish
same word

child → children
special ending!

woman → women
mouse → mice
change the vowel

person → people
different word!

---

1 How many are there?

> boy bus fish foot knife leaf
> person sheep shelf watch woman

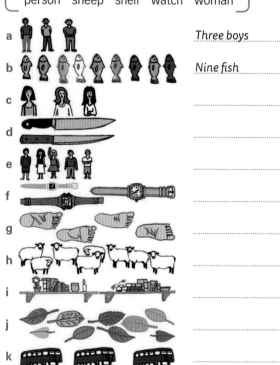

a *Three boys*

b *Nine fish*

c ....

d ....

e ....

f ....

g ....

h ....

i ....

j ....

k ....

2 Correct the mistakes.

a Go upstairs and clean your ~~tooth.~~ *teeth*
b How many child do you have? ....
c Please put these knife on the table. ....
d We went to some wonderful party last week!
   ....
e There are lots of beautiful tree in this forest.
   ....
f Where are the English-Chinese dictionary?
   ....
g William bought twelve egg and six sausage.
   ....
h I have three credit card and I spend too much
   money! ....
i How many English teacher work in your school?
   ....
j The washing machine are in the basement.
   ....
k I always buy all my train ticket online. ....
l Jane met lots of interesting person at the meeting.
   ....
m This computer game is so hard! I've only got
   two life left! ....

More practice

Indefinite article

vowel sound		consonant sound	
an orange book	an idea	a green book	a towel
an egg	an animal	a field	a cat

a/an = one
She's got a cat = She's got one cat
Can you stay for a minute? = Can you stay for one minute?

⚠ 'hour' starts with a vowel sound! = *an hour.*
a university, an MBA, a one-year course, an LCD television, a European

Use *a / an* to say ... what work people do
Shari's an accountant.
I'm a software engineer.

or what something is
That's an express train.
This is a discount card.
A Kindle is an electronic book.

---

1 Write *a* or *an*.

a ___a___ a house
b ___an___ argument
c .... window
d .... computer
e .... hour
f .... Italian meal
g .... insect
h .... yellow plant
i .... university
j .... European country
k .... yoga teacher
l .... English teacher

2 What are the everyday objects? Work out the anagrams.

a UCSEPAAN ___It's a saucepan.___
b GGE ....
c PLAPE ....
d NOIR ....
e FARSC ....
f OLETBT ....
g GANHDAB ....

3 What work do they do? Work out the anagrams.

a CAEDNR ___He's a dancer.___
b ROOTCD ....
c LOTIP ....
d TSAIRT ....
e LAEETTH ....

4 Write *a* or *an*.

a I bought ___a___ guidebook in the museum.
b What .... beautiful mountain!
c There's .... fresh apple on the table.
d Look! I think there's .... elephant behind that tree.
e She wrote .... interesting story about .... angry office worker.
f I can't make the omelette. I need .... box of eggs, ... onion and .... tomato.
g Is there .... exit near here?
h My husband's .... pilot and I'm .... engineer.
i Could I have .... receipt, please?

More practice

Decide whether to use *a*, *an* or *the*

Indefinite and definite articles

general = 'a'

specific = 'the'

i.e. you know exactly which one I'm talking about

Can I borrow a dictionary?

We've got a new printer.

That's the book I need!

The printer's broken.

She doesn't want a specific dictionary. Any dictionary will be OK.

It's not important exactly which one they got.

We know which book he is talking about. It **IS** important which one.

She is talking about the printer in the room – not any other

We use 'the' when there is only one of these things.

We also use 'the' when everyone already knows what you are talking about.

the Sun   the Moon   the sky

the bus station   the garden

the kitchen   the countryside

We saw a great film last night. It's called *Ikiru*.

I've never heard of it! What's the film about?

When something is **new** in the conversation, the first time it's mentioned: use *a / an*.

When something has been **mentioned earlier** in the conversation: use *the*.

So ... we walked until we came to an old house. **The** building was completely empty. No lights.

1 Complete the sentences. Use *a, an* or *the*.

a Tim's __*a*__ taxi driver. He lives quite near my house, in __*the*__ town centre.

b I'd like _____ glass of orange juice and _____ slice of chocolate cake.

c 'We moved to _____ new office.' 'Really? Where is _____ office?'

d I want to send Tim _____ email. Could you tell me _____ address?

e 'I've got _____ great idea!' 'What?' 'Let's find _____ small restaurant in _____ countryside and have _____ romantic meal!'

f He told the children _____ frightening bedtime story about _____ wolf.

g 'Have you got _____ car?' 'Yes. It's _____ Volkswagen.'

h Violet is _____ accountant. She is _____ only accountant that I know!

i That was _____ great holiday. I thought _____ beach was wonderful.

j 'Could you lend me _____ calculator?' 'Yes. Look. There's a calculator on _____ table next to _____ door.'

k 'It's _____ lovely day! _____ sun is shining! _____ weather forecast is good. Let's go to _____ park and have _____ swim.'

l Sheila works in _____ old bookshop next to _____ bus station in the town centre.

m _____ TV in the living room doesn't work. We need to buy _____ new one.

n I can't do _____ last question in this exercise!

o **Angus:** Are you waiting for _____ bus or _____ tram?
   Julia: _____ bus. Aah, that's _____ bus I want!

p **Susan:** Do you live in _____ flat or _____ house?
   Mary: _____ flat.
   Susan: I live in _____ flat too.

2 Complete the story. Use *a, an* or *the*.

Angelina Pepper (Secret Agent XX5) saw an old building on the other side of a field. She ran across __*the*__ ^a field and hid behind a tall fence. She looked up at __*the*__ ^b sky. It was nearly dark and _____ ^c sun was low. She looked carefully at _____ ^d building, trying to spot _____ ^e open window. Ah! There! On _____ ^f first floor!

She stood up and walked away from the fence, moving slowly towards _____ ^g building. She looked up at _____ ^h window. 'I've got _____ ⁱ long rope in my backpack,' she thought. She opened _____ ^j backpack and took out _____ ^k rope. She threw it up at the window. When it was safe, she climbed up.

She saw _____ ^l large room. Inside _____ ^m room she could see _____ ⁿ piano and _____ ^o brightly-coloured parrot, fast asleep in _____ ^p cage. She walked over to _____ ^q piano, sat down and started to play _____ ^r pretty tune. _____ ^s parrot woke up and called 'Biscuits. Biscuits'. Angelina heard footsteps at _____ ^t other end of _____ ^u room. Someone walked over to _____ ^v cage. Angelina imagined that he was giving _____ ^w biscuit to the parrot.

Then she heard _____ ^x voice right behind her.

'Well, well, well, Ms Pepper. You have found me! Please don't turn around. I have _____ ^y gun in my hand.' Angelina smiled. 'Do you like _____ ^z music?' she asked.

Decide when *the* isn't needed

Omission of **a, an, the**

---

no article in front of...

proper names

Ø James

Ø Philadelphia

Ø Harvard

uncountable nouns and plural countable nouns about general things

I love Ø rice!

I enjoy Ø frightening films.

We never buy Ø potatoes.

This is beautiful Ø music!

 When we mean 'all' or 'in general'.

I don't like dogs (= all dogs, everywhere).
I don't like the dogs (= the dogs in a particular place).

Chips are delicious (= all chips – in general).
The chips are delicious (= the particular chips we are talking about).

Reggae music is popular all over the world (= reggae music in general).
The reggae music is too loud (= the particular music in this place, now).

school subjects, sports

Greg hates Ø Chemistry.

Tommy loves Ø football.

some places you go to for a reason

I start Ø school at 8.30.

Meryl's at Ø work.

Jack's still in Ø bed.

He left Ø university last year.

She's in Ø hospital.

Let's go to Ø town.

Fergus is at Ø home.

The family are in Ø church at the moment.

If we are thinking of the building ...
The tourists are looking at the church.
Where's the hospital?

and
the cinema, the bank, the station, the library, the swimming pool, the sports centre, the shopping mall, the town centre, the bus station

---

1 People are talking about things and people that they really like. All the sentences begin *I really love ...* Underline the correct words.

I really love ...

a Susana / the Susana
b picture / the picture
c New York / the New York
d tennis / the tennis
e Princess / the Princess
f town centre / the town centre
g Peter and Sara / the Peter and Sara
h new car / the new car
i home / the home
j Moon / the Moon
k song / the song
l Geography / the Geography

2 Write *the* or Ø (= no article).

a I love __the__ music in this concert.
b What kind of __Ø__ music do you like?
c My son, Ben, is at .... university, but my daughters are still at .... school.
d Where's .... hospital?
e Mike is in .... hospital for three days.
f When do you finish .... work each day?
g Chen goes to .... work at 5.30 every morning.
h I love .... town centre, but I hate .... shopping mall.
i It's very late. Stuart's going to .... bed now.
j I'd like to buy .... bed in the shop window.
k I love .... carrots, but I hate .... peas.
l David is very interested in .... ships.
m David thinks .... ship is beautiful.

More practice

so that • infinitive of purpose

I saved my money : to buy a new moped.

| what I did | infinitive | why I did it |

Oliver got a new passport : so that he could go to South Africa.

why he did it

| what he did | so that + would/could |

can/could and will/would

Taylor borrowed $50. Now she **can** buy new shoes

Taylor borrowed $50 so that she **could** buy new shoes.

Terry has left his job. Now he **will** have more time with his children.

Terry left his job so that he **would** have more time with his children.

Question	Answer
Why did you go to the market?	To get some tomatoes.
Why are you going to the market?	
Why are you going to go to the market?	

past, present or future!

Question	Answer
Why did Cherry go into the garden?	To pick some flowers.
Why did Jake phone his father?	To ask for advice.
Why did they go to India?	So that they could visit their family.
She drove very fast! Why?	So that we would be on time.

1 Match the questions with the answers.

a Why did you go to the library?
b Why did you climb the tree?
c Why did you learn French?
d Why did you buy a new cooker?
e Why did you turn the TV off?
f Why did you set your alarm for 5 a.m.?
g Why did the chicken cross the road?

1 To make my own bread.
2 To borrow a book about Antarctica.
3 So that I wouldn't be late for my exam this morning.
4 To get my son's ball.
5 To get to the other side!
6 So that I could hear what my mum was saying.
7 So that I could teach it to my five-year-old!

2 Complete the sentences. Use the words in brackets.

a Andy went to the supermarket ... (get some fruit)
to *get some fruit.*

b We came home early ... (see Grandma)
so that *we could see Grandma.*

c Paul borrowed £20 ... (buy some concert tickets)
to ....

d Mike phoned Janice ... (tell her about the prize)
so that ....

e Ronnie wanted a password ... (open the program)
to ....

f Magda went the gym at 6 a.m. ... (do more exercise)
so that ....

3 *INTERNET* QUIZ

Why do people do these things?

a Every year millions of tourists visit Agra ...
to visit the Taj Mahal.

b Lots of people visit Chengdu Research Base ...
....

c In 1959 Barack Obama's father travelled from Kenya to the USA ...
....

d People learn CPR ...
....

Imperatives • Let's

Tell people what to do ...

Put the towels in the drawer.

Close the windows.

Go to the bathroom.

Cut up the carrots.

Come here! Wait!

Stop!

Tell people what not to do ...

Don't feed the fish!

Don't do that!

Don't make so much noise

Don't disturb the baby!

Don't wait! Don't go!

Don't stop!

Tell people what not to do with *Don't* ...

Don't unplug the fridge.

Don't lose your temper!   *Don't worry!*

Don't be angry!

We can also warn people ...

Don't talk to any strangers!   *Don't be late.*

Make orders more polite with *Could you* ... or *please*.

Could you call me after ten?

Wait here, please.

Could you tidy these books, please?

Be quiet, please!

Offer people good wishes with *Have* ...

Have a great time!   *Have a safe journey!*

Have a lovely party!   *Have a nice day!*

Offer food and drink with *Have* ...

Have a cookie!   *Have some cola!*

Have a taste!   *Have a slice!*

Make suggestions about what you can do with *Let's* ...

Let's start.

Let's go outside.

Let's have a game before dinner.

Let's sit down for a few minutes.

I'm tired! Let's take a taxi.

---

1 Choose the best expression from the box for each situation.

> Be quiet!   Come back!   ~~Come in!~~
> Don't forget!   Don't lose your temper!
> Go away!   Have fun!   Hurry up!   Say cheese!
> Slow down!   Tell me!   Wait here.

a Someone knocks on your office door. You say
   '*Come in!*'

b A strange dog is running around you. It's very
   annoying. You say ....

c Your teacher says he can discuss your exam
   results with you at 2 p.m. He knows that
   sometimes you don't remember to do things. He
   says ....

d A class of students is making a lot of noise. The
   teacher calls ....

e Your train will leave in two minutes. Your friend is
   walking very slowly. You say ....

f You are a receptionist. Someone has arrived
   30 minutes early for an interview. You say
   ....

g A man was very rude to your best friend. She
   looks very angry. You think she is going to shout at
   him. You say ....

h Your friend says that she has some amazing news.
   You say ....

i You are taking a photo of your children. You say
   ....

j Your friend is talking very fast and you can't
   understand her story. You say ....

k You want to talk to a small child, but he is walking
   away from you. You call ....

l Your daughter is going to a party. You say
   ....

2 Look at the pictures. Tell people what to do. Use the verbs in the box.

> be   click   close   disturb   feed   look   ~~open~~   ~~park~~   stop   take

a

Open your book.

b

Don't park here.

g

h

c

d

i

j

e

f

3 What can you and your friends do? Look at the pictures and make suggestions.

a

Let's have an ice cream!

b

c

d

e

f

4 Read the situations. What do the people say? Use the expressions in the box.

> Let's ask!   Let's get some food!
> Let's go back!   ~~Let's go!~~   Let's start!
> Let's try again!   Let's wait!   Let's walk!

a The Green family are going to the theatre. Mr Green is waiting for everyone to get ready. He thinks they'll be late. He calls out *'Let's go!'*

b All the company managers are sitting round the table at the beginning of an important meeting. The boss looks at the clock and says

c John and Margaret are in a shopping centre. John doesn't know which floor the shoe shop is on. Margaret sees an Information Desk and says

d Susie and Tammy are walking to school together. Tammy suddenly says 'Oh! I left my bag at home!' Susie says

e The young children couldn't add 7 and 7. 'Don't worry!' the teacher said

f Mike and Jeffrey have just missed a bus. The next one is in 40 minutes! Mike says

g ... but Jeffrey says 'No. I'm tired!

h ... 'OK!' says Mike. 'But I'm hungry!

I can ... Use countable and mass nouns

Countable and uncountable nouns

1 2 3 4

| things = countable | stuff = uncountable |

We can count some things ...

I've got	eight mice.	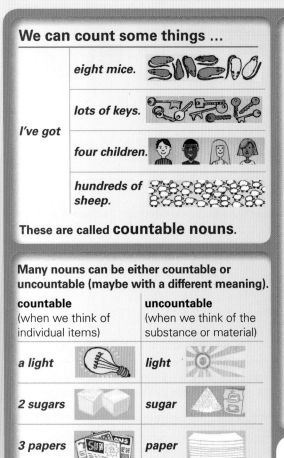
	lots of keys.	
	four children.	
	hundreds of sheep.	

These are called **countable nouns**.

Many nouns can be either countable or uncountable (maybe with a different meaning).

countable (when we think of individual items)	uncountable (when we think of the substance or material)
a light	light
2 sugars	sugar
3 papers	paper

We can't count some things ...

I've got ...	some rice.	(food)
	some jam.	
	some milk.	(liquid)
	some water.	
	some metal.	(material)
	some cotton.	
	some news.	(abstract ideas)
	some information.	
I enjoy ...	sport.	(general activities)
	work.	

We can't normally use these nouns with *a/an* or with a number, e.g. ✗ *an information* ✗ *three news* ✗ *seven rice*.

We can use *some*, e.g. *some light, some chocolate*.

They do not normally have plurals, e.g. ✗ *some informations* ✗ *some rices*.

These are called **mass** or **uncountable nouns**.

1 Decide if the words are (C) countable or (U) uncountable or (C/U) both. If a word is countable, write the plural.

a	information	(U)	j	orange juice	
b	lake	(C) lakes	k	ice	
c	pen		l	£10 note	
d	rice		m	money	
e	tea		n	news	
f	tooth		o	newspaper	
g	person		p	paper	
h	sunshine		q	coat	
i	happiness		r	father	

2 Write *a* (if the word is countable) or *some* (if it is uncountable).

a I bought ___some___ salt because we don't have any at home.

b Sergei drove here in ___a___ minibus.

c It's very quiet in here! Can you put on _____ music, please?

d I want _____ newspaper to find out what the football score is.

e Did the teacher give us _____ homework for tonight?

f I'm really hungry! I need _____ food!

g This is _____ horrible meal!

h Meryl needs _____ help. Can you call her?

3 Change one word to correct the mistake in each sentence.

  a I love eating ~~pastas~~. *pasta*

  b She bought ~~a~~ lovely furniture. *some*

  c Have you done your homeworks? ....

  d She gave Betty some very important advices.

  ....

  e I don't like the weathers today. ....

  f I heard a really interesting news. ....

  g Have you got any informations about train times to London? ....

  h We had funs at the carnival. ....

  i He bought some flours at the supermarket.

  ....

  j You have beautiful hairs. ....

4 THE TOUGH ONE

Complete the sentences with the words in brackets. Make plurals where necessary.

  a We can count ....*suitcases*.... but not ....*luggage*..... (luggage; suitcase)

  b We can count .... but not .... (newspaper; news)

  c We can count .... but not .... (traffic; car)

  d We can count .... but not .... (exercise; homework)

  e We can count .... but not .... (chair; furniture)

  f We can count .... but not .... (money; coin)

  g We can count .... but not .... (weather; cloud)

I can ... Ask people what they would like (food, drink, etc.)

a/an/some

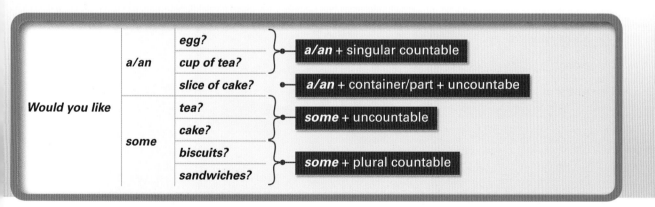

Would you like	a/an	egg?	a/an + singular countable
		cup of tea?	
		slice of cake?	a/an + container/part + uncountabe
	some	tea?	some + uncountable
		cake?	
		biscuits?	some + plural countable
		sandwiches?	

1 Complete the questions with *a*, *an* or *some*.

  a Would you like ....*some*.... water?

  b Would you like .... banana?

  c Would you like .... bananas?

  d Would you like .... bread?

  e Would you like .... slice of bread?

  f Would you like .... medicine?

  g Would you like .... cup of hot chocolate?

  h Would you like .... food?

  i Would you like .... cookie?

  j Would you like .... cough sweets?

  k Would you like .... information?

  l Would you like .... bottle of cola?

  m Would you like to listen to .... music?

More practice

We can't normally count uncountable nouns (*~~five toothpastes, seven meats~~*).

But we can count containers (*bottles, cans, packets*, etc.) or weights, parts and pieces (*a slice of, a kilo of, a piece of*, etc.).

✓ **two bottles of milk**
✓ **five tubes of toothpaste**
✓ **seven slices of meat**

Sometimes we don't say the container.
Two milks, please. = Two glasses/packets/bottles of milk, please.

1 Match the words (a–o) with the pictures (1–15). Then match them with a food, liquid, material, etc. (A–O). (Different answers may be possible.)

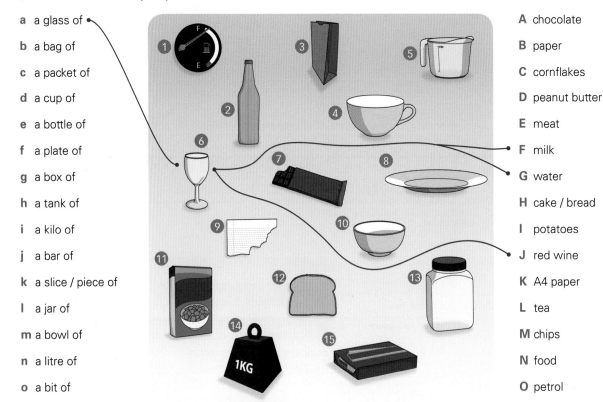

a a glass of		**A** chocolate
b a bag of		**B** paper
c a packet of		**C** cornflakes
d a cup of		**D** peanut butter
e a bottle of		**E** meat
f a plate of		**F** milk
g a box of		**G** water
h a tank of		**H** cake / bread
i a kilo of		**I** potatoes
j a bar of		**J** red wine
k a slice / piece of		**K** A4 paper
l a jar of		**L** tea
m a bowl of		**M** chips
n a litre of		**N** food
o a bit of		**O** petrol

2 Look back at the words in **1**. Which can be used with these items? (Different answers may be possible.)

a Mmm! That was a delicious ....*cup*........ of coffee.

b I didn't eat just one piece! I ate a whole .... of chocolate!

c We need some tomatoes and carrots. Oh, and could you get a five-kilo .... of potatoes?

d When the Smiths arrived at the party, they gave their hostess a .... of red wine.

e Before you start your journey, make sure your car has a full .... of petrol.

f Is the photocopier empty? I think there's a .... of A4 paper on my desk.

g On the breakfast table I saw a few rolls, a slice of ham and a .... of peanut butter.

h 'I'm giving up smoking' he said and threw his .... of cigarettes in the bin.

i After the long run, she was very thirsty and drank half a .... of water.

j Could I have a .... of beef, please?

More practice

some/any

We often use *some* in statements and *any* in questions and negatives:

I've got some oil.

Have you got any oil?

I haven't got any oil.

But we can also use *some* in offers and questions:

Would you like some oil?

Have you got some oil?

SQUEAK!

Have you got any cash? uncountable noun

Have you got any ideas? plural countable noun

We don't need to repeat a noun.

I made these cookies. Would you like some ~~cookies~~?

This green tea is delicious. Where can I buy some ~~green tea~~?

There aren't any pens here – but Anna has some ~~pens~~ *in the study.*

Our flat has got two balconies, but their house hasn't got any ~~balconies~~.

Pete had some lemonade, but I didn't want any ~~lemonade~~.

1 Complete the sentences with *some* or *any*. (In some sentences, both may be possible.)

a I need ___some___ batteries for this old torch.
b Have you written _____ new songs today?
c We drove through the park for an hour, but didn't see _____ zebras.
d Would you like to have _____ fizzy water?
e Sarah didn't need _____ help with her essay.
f Can I borrow _____ cash?
g The teacher hasn't got _____ more worksheets.
h The stewardess offered the passengers _____ lemon sweets.
i There were _____ very old magazines on the table.
j I'm sorry. I haven't got _____ more glue.

2 Complete the sentences. Use the verbs in the box (in the right tense) and *some* or *any*.

> catch cook ~~have~~ iron
> pick remember ~~try~~ want

a Mark wanted to borrow some money, but I didn't *have any.*
b Terri's curry smelt delicious. When she wasn't watching, I *tried some.*
d Sam was fishing all morning. He saw lots of fish, but he couldn't _____ .

e Harvey didn't have any shirts to wear so I
_____ .

f The wild flowers in this field are beautiful. Let's
_____ .

g Jessica said she liked fried eggs so I
_____ .

h Wendy asked me if I knew any Japanese words, but I couldn't _____ .

i Susie bought some ice cream, but I didn't
_____ .

3 INTERNET QUIZ 🔍

Complete the sentences. Use *some* or *any* and a word from the box. Then decide if the sentence is true or false.

> exercises ~~footprints~~ information
> islands sharks skyscrapers

a There are *some footprints* on the Moon.   *True*
b On the UN website, you can also read
_____ in Chinese, Arabic
and Russian.   _____
c _____ lay eggs, but others
have live babies.   _____
d There aren't _____ in the
Pacific Ocean where humans can live.   _____
e This book hasn't got _____
about uncountable nouns   _____
f _____ on Earth are taller
than Everest.   _____

I can ... Ask and answer about quantities

much/many/a lot of/lots of

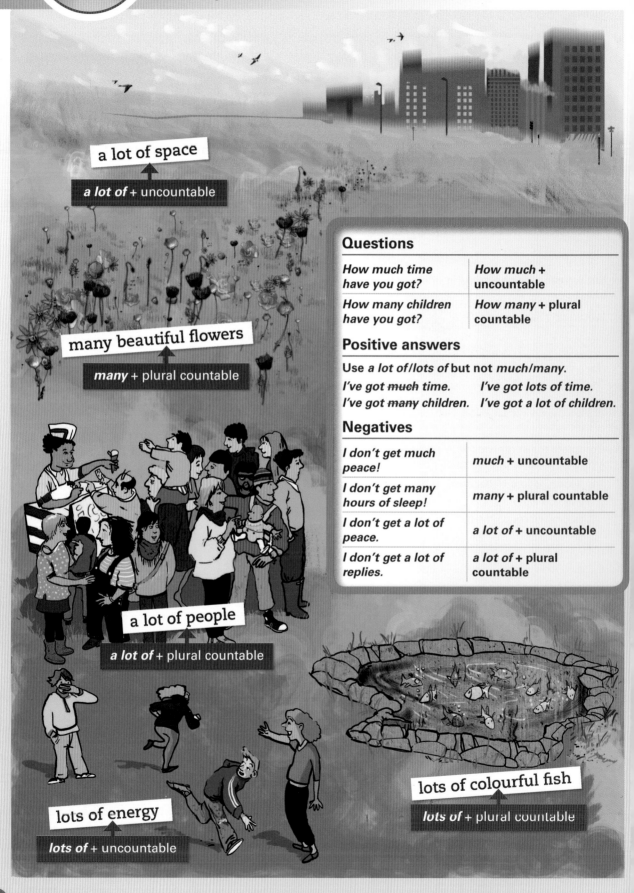

a lot of space

a lot of + uncountable

many beautiful flowers

many + plural countable

a lot of people

a lot of + plural countable

lots of energy

lots of + uncountable

lots of colourful fish

lots of + plural countable

Questions

How much time have you got?	How much + uncountable
How many children have you got?	How many + plural countable

Positive answers

Use *a lot of/lots of* but not *much/many*.

I've got ~~much~~ time.   I've got lots of time.
I've got ~~many~~ children.   I've got a lot of children.

Negatives

I don't get much peace!	*much* + uncountable
I don't get many hours of sleep!	*many* + plural countable
I don't get a lot of peace.	*a lot of* + uncountable
I don't get a lot of replies.	*a lot of* + plural countable

1 In each pair, one question begins *How much* and one begins *How many*. Which is which?

a *How many*.......... cars did you see after midnight?
   How much.......... traffic was there after midnight?

b .... food did they cook?
   .... potatoes did they cook?

c .... drinks shall I order?
   .... juice shall I bring?

d .... work is there at the factory?
   .... jobs are there at the factory?

e .... information did she give you?
   .... facts did she tell you?

f .... dollars did you make on eBay?
   .... profit did you make on eBay?

g .... oxygen is there on the Moon?
   .... rings are there around Saturn?

h .... bills did he pay?
   .... tax did he pay?

i .... advice did he give you?
   .... suggestions did he give you?

j .... schools are there in this district?
   .... education do most children receive?

k .... songs will they sing tonight?
   .... music will they play tonight?

l .... electric guitars do you have?
   .... electricity do you use each month?

m .... accommodation is there?
   .... people live in these apartments?

2 Make sentences with *much*.

a Pilar only drank a little tea.
   Pilar didn't *drink much tea.*........................

b Joseph only watched TV for a few minutes.
   Joseph didn't ....

c The receptionist gave us almost no information.
   The receptionist didn't ....

d Stewart only ate very little dessert.
   Stewart didn't ....

e Angie had very little money in her purse.
   Angie didn't ....

f There was a very small amount of milk in the fridge.
   There wasn't ....

g George had only a short time to practise.
   George didn't ....

3 *A lot of* is correct in each sentence. In which sentences could you use *much* instead?

a

I have a lot of books.

✗ *much is not possible*

b

I don't have a lot of money.

✓ *much is possible*

c

I have a lot of children.

d

They have a lot of toys.

e

I don't get a lot of peace and quiet.

f

I don't have a lot of patience.

g
My wife, though, has a lot of patience.

h
I don't get a lot of sleep.

4 Use the word pool to make six sentences and questions.

a   the   how   of
Polly   bears   sandwiches   honey
see   make   made   eat   ate
do   doesn't   don't   did   didn't
much   lot   lots   many

....
....
....
....

1 Complete the table.

Adjective	Adverb	Adjective	Adverb
a slow	*slowly*	**g** good	
b *warm*	warmly	**h**	honestly
c happy		**i** formal	
d	correctly	**j** gentle	
e fast		**k**	fluently
f	violently		

2 Underline the correct word.

a Why is this bus so _slow_ / slowly? We're going to be late.

b This bus is going very slow / _slowly_. We're going to be late.

c You cook Indian food really *good* / *well*!

d This meal is very *good* / *well*.

e Jaroslav speaks English *perfect* / *perfectly*.

f Mechteld speaks *perfect* / *perfectly* English.

g Sami can't write good English, but he speaks *fluent* / *fluently*.

h You're *strong* / *strongly*! Can you help me carry this box, please?

i I shouted *angry* / *angrily* at them.

j The librarian asked us to talk *quiet* / *quietly*.

Adverbs tell us *how* people do things (e.g. *loudly, hungrily, beautifully, suddenly, nicely, easily*).

 adjective

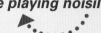 adverb

I've got three noisy children!

The children are playing noisily.

Adjectives tell us more about **nouns**.

Adverbs tell us more about **verbs**.

What are the children like?

They're noisy!

How are the children playing?

Noisily!

	adjective	adverb
+ ly	quick	→ quickly
	excited	→ excitedly
	perfect	→ perfectly
	hopeful	→ hopefully

	adjective	adverb
y → i + ly	happy	→ happily
	hungry	→ hungrily
	thirsty	→ thirstily

		adjective	adverb
le → ly		terrible	→ terribly
same word		fast	→ fast
different word		good	→ well

Some adjectives don't have an adverb:

big	→ ✗
ugly	→ ✗
young	→ ✗
frightened	→ ✗

Sometimes we use a phrase instead of an adverb:

friendly → in a friendly way

---

3 Complete the text with the words in the box.

carefully   correctly   gently   ~~honestly~~
perfectly   ~~well~~   wrongly

OK Jacinta. I'm going to talk to you _honestly_ ª.
You're not playing ___ _well_ ᵇ today! Look at me
and watch ___ ᶜ! This is how to hold the
racket ___ ᵈ. You are holding it ___ ᵉ
and you're hitting the ball too ___ ᶠ. ... So,
try again! ... Great! You hit that one ___ ᵍ.

4 **THE TOUGH ONE**

Answer the questions in your own words. Use a
dictionary or the internet to help you.

How do you ...

a drive? _Fast but carefully._
b do yoga? _Quietly and peacefully._
c make fresh mayonnaise? ___
d play volleyball (or other ball games)?
___
e speak English? ___
f write English? ___
g sing? ___
h dance in a disco? ___
i do clothes shopping? ___

There was .../There were ...

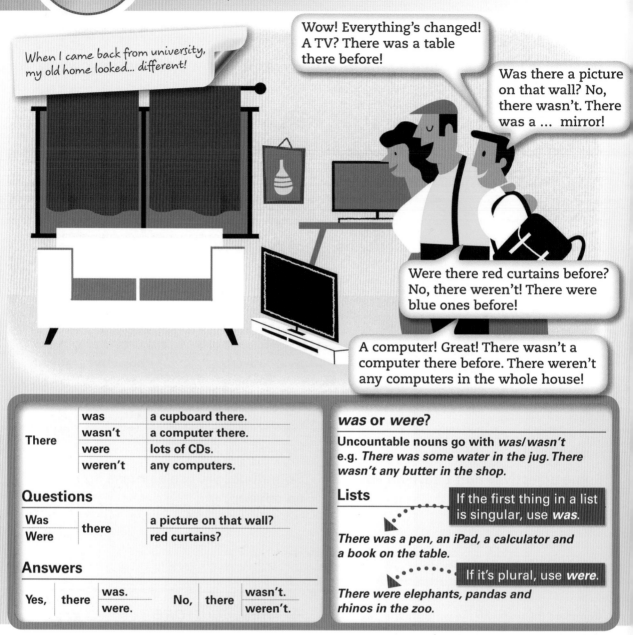

When I came back from university, my old home looked... different!

Wow! Everything's changed! A TV? There was a table there before!

Was there a picture on that wall? No, there wasn't. There was a ... mirror!

Were there red curtains before? No, there weren't! There were blue ones before!

A computer! Great! There wasn't a computer there before. There weren't any computers in the whole house!

	was	a cupboard there.
There	wasn't	a computer there.
	were	lots of CDs.
	weren't	any computers.

Questions

Was	there	a picture on that wall?
Were		red curtains?

Answers

Yes,	there	was. / were.	No,	there	wasn't. / weren't.

was or were?

Uncountable nouns go with *was/wasn't* e.g. *There was some water in the jug. There wasn't any butter in the shop.*

Lists

> If the first thing in a list is singular, use *was*.

There was a pen, an iPad, a calculator and a book on the table.

> If it's plural, use *were*.

There were elephants, pandas and rhinos in the zoo.

1 Complete the sentences with *There was* or *There were*.

a   *There were*   a lot of people at the party.

b   .... some interesting ideas at the meeting.

c   .... some good information in that app.

d   .... a long taxi queue outside the theatre.

e   .... only three good apples in the bag.

f   .... a lovely beach next to the hotel.

g   .... a ball, a teddy bear, a train and a drum in the toy box.

h   .... singers, dancers, magicians and comedians in the show.

2 Complete the questions with *Was there* or *Were there*.

a   *Was there*   a light in the cellar?

b   .... any tourists at the castle?

c   .... a good answer to question 3(d)?

d   .... any nuts in that cake?

e   .... any sugar in that cake?

f   .... any Maths homework last night?

g   .... any Maths questions in last night's homework?

More practice

will (for decisions)

Don't worry, young man!

He has just decided what to do.

I'll clean the floor.

I'll pick up all the rubbish.

I'll answer the phone.

I'll save the cat.

And ... I'll explain everything to your mum.

	help	you with your homework.
	make	supper tonight.
I'll	get	it.
	finish	this later.
	call	my boss now.
	do	it tomorrow.

'll is the usual form. Only use *will* if you want to make it sound like a very strong decision.

stressed → I **will** pass this horrible exam!
I **will** tidy my room!
I **will** give up smoking!

When people hear a doorbell or a phone ringing, they sometimes say 'I'll get it'. This means 'I'll answer it'.

When you decide to buy something in a shop, you can say 'I'll take it.'

1 Match what A says (a–g) with B's replies (1–7).

a Does anyone want the last piece of cake?
b My bike's broken. I need to get to the station.
c Normal price £4. Special offer today – only £1 each!
d What's your phone number?
e This plate is still dirty.
f I'm not free until this afternoon.
g When does our train leave?

1 I'll check on the internet.
2 I'll text it to you!
3 OK. I'll meet you at 2.00.
4 I'll have it!
5 I'll give you a lift!
6 I'll do it again.
7 I'll take three!

2 How can you help these people? Make offers using the words in the box.

> change the batteries   get it
> give her some food   Google it
> lend you some   ~~look for it~~

a I've lost my handbag.

b I haven't got enough money for lunch.

I'll look for it.

c The baby is crying.

d I can hear the front doorbell.

e Do you know what the capital of Iceland is?

f The TV remote control doesn't work.

3 ABOUT YOU

Marty has decided five things she'll do next week.

I'll learn twenty new English verbs.
I'll get up early every day.
I'll do more exercise.
I'll learn how to make Caesar Salad.
I'll talk more politely to my mother!

Now decide five things <u>you'll</u> do next week.

More practice

I can ... Say what I think will happen

will (for future) • Other functions of **will**

Past **I was**

Present **I am**

Future **I will be**

Future facts and predictions

There'll be drinks before the meeting.
When will the film start?
Will the shop close at 5.30?
I won't be home till late.
I think Peter will get married in April!
They'll be in Brussels all week.
Will humans live on Mars?

Promises

He'll give you the money tomorrow.
I'll call you tonight!

Warnings and threats

Careful! You'll get paint on your fingers!
Stop or I'll shoot!

Asking for help

Will you show me what to do?
Will someone pick me up after the meeting?

Invitations

Will you come round on Thursday?	Thank you! I'd love to!
Will you join us for lunch?	Thank you, but I'm afraid I can't.

Offers to help

I'll get your bag for you = Shall I get your bag for you?	Thanks! That's very kind of you.
I'll get you a ticket = Shall I get you a ticket?	No, thanks. I can do it myself.

I/You/He/She/It/We/They	will	do ... see ... get ... buy ...

Yes/no questions

Will	I/you/he/she/it/we/they	sing ... cook ... walk ... watch ...	?

Short answers

Use *will* if you are sure.	Use *might* if you aren't sure.

Yes,	I/you/he/she/it/we/they	will / might.
No,	I/you/he/she/it/we/they	won't / might not.

Wh- questions

When How Why What Where Who	will	I/you/he/she/it/we/they	meet ... go ... explain call ...	?

Negatives

I/You/He/She/It/We/They	won't (will not)	come ... say ... promise ... eat ...

Use *I think, probably* or *definitely* to say how sure you are.

I think I'll be at the office until 6 o'clock.
Brazil will definitely win the World Cup!
The economy will probably improve next year.

Use *I don't think + will* to say that you think something will not happen.

I don't think Mary will get the new job.

See you soon/later means the same as '*I'll see you soon/later'.*

---

1 Which sentences are
- asking for help?
- an offer to help?
- a promise?
- a warning or threat?

a Don't worry! I'll be home before midnight. ....*a promise*........

b Sit down. I'll tidy the room. ....

c Give me that chocolate or I'll tell Mummy! ....

d Will you get a newspaper from the local shop, please? ....

e I'll tell you the answer tomorrow. ....

f I'll get you some aspirin. ....

2 Complete the sentences with *'ll/will* or *won't*.

a Jill said that the party ......*will*...... start at 7. I ...*won't*... be able to get there until about 9 o'clock.

b 'I think that in the future everyone .... travel in flying cars!' 'No, they .... !'

c Mum! George .... give me my doll! Mum! .... you tell him to give it back?

d We .... meet everyone at the ceremony. Afterwards, we .... stay long because we need to drive straight home.

e The factory .... close in July. After that, I .... have a job!

f '............ you have some more dessert?' 'Oh, no thank you! I .... eat any more! It was really delicious, but I'm full up!'

g 'Dad! The TV's broken. It .... switch on!' 'OK. Give me the control. I .... try.'

h Gordon .... be in India next week. He said that he .... phone us because it's very expensive.

3 **ABOUT YOU**

First make questions about your future life with *will*. Then give true, short answers. Write *Yes, I will/might* or *No, I won't/might not*.

a visit / lots of foreign countries
Will you visit lots of foreign countries? Yes, I will.

b live / a foreign country

c study / another language

d celebrate / your next birthday

e become / very rich

4 Offer to help using *Shall ...* . Use the verbs in the box.

> change   lend   ~~open~~   tell   tidy

a The window is closed.
Shall I open the window?

b The table is a mess.

c Ruth doesn't know the answer.

d The TV is on the wrong channel.

e Sam has no money.

5 **ABOUT YOU**

Write some of your own ideas about the future. Use *'ll/will/won't*.

a Robots *will do all the boring work.*

b Humans .... other planets.

c Computers ....

d .... books ....

e I ....

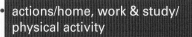

actions/home, work & study/ physical activity

Cheryl did five different jobs last year.

Kate does the housework every morning.

do

Have you done any exercise today?

I'm doing the spreadsheet now.

cooking/creating/building/ communication

Cheryl made some cakes last night.

Kate's making a new notice to put in the staffroom.

make

I've made a Lego model of a plane!

The factory makes tablet computers.

everyday actions / eating & drinking / other actions

Cheryl had a long bath after she got up.

Kate's had five cups of coffee!

have

Can you call later? I'm having dinner!

Let's have a break!

Some nouns go with *do*. Some go with *make*. Some go with *have*. Often there is no good reason why we use *do, make* or *have*. You just have to learn which is the right verb!

do		make		have	
Home	**Business**	**Cooking**	**Business**	**Everyday actions**	**Fun**
the shopping	*business with someone*	*dinner*	*a profit*	*a shower*	*a party*
the ironing	*a deal with someone*	*a cup of tea*	*an appointment*	*a chat*	*a picnic*
the cleaning		**Communication**	*a suggestion*	*a look*	*a good laugh*
the cooking		*a phone call*	**Problems**	*a bad dream*	*a holiday*
School		*a complaint*	*a noise*	*a sleep*	*a good time*
your homework		*a request*	*a mess*	*a cigarette*	*a nice afternoon*
an essay		*an excuse*	*trouble*	*a meal*	**Medical**
an exam		*a comment*		*a think*	*a cold*
an exercise		**School**		**Eating & drinking**	*a check-up*
an English course		*a note*		*a glass of cola*	*a scan*
a project		*a mistake*		*breakfast*	*an illness*
		a list		*a drink of water*	
		a decision			

Common expressions

Can you do me a favour? (= Can you help me?)
Make up your mind! (= Decide!)
Would you like to have a go? (= Would you like to try?)
I want to make some money. (= I want to earn some money.)
Don't make a fuss! (= Don't complain, make a noise and be difficult!)

Common mistakes

I made **took** a photograph of Spiderman.

I made **did** my homework at lunchtime!

I saw **had** a wonderful dream last night.

Oops! I did **made** a mistake.

1 Complete the sentences with *have*, *make* or *do*.

a I'm going upstairs to __have__ a bath.
b Did you __make__ a shopping list?
c Don't forget to .... your homework!
d Would you like to .... a drink? I've got orange juice or lemonade.
e Will you .... some food for the baby?
f What are you going to .... this evening? See a film or go dancing?
g I hope I don't .... a terrible mistake in my interview!
h Mary is frightened that she will .... a bad dream again tonight.
i What does this factory ....? Cars or buses?
j Hello? Is that the dentist? I'd like to .... an appointment for next Thursday.
k After you have read the text please .... Exercises 7 and 8.
l Do you want to .... a look at the new baby? He's gorgeous!
m I think that the Indian office will .... a profit for the first time this year.

2 Underline the correct word.

a Ben and Danielle *had / made* a long chat last night.
b Next year I'm going to *do / make* a Japanese conversation course.
c I'm sorry, Jane can't come to the party. She *has / makes* a terrible cold.
d I *did / made* a model of a spaceship for homework last week.
e Nik's at the customer service desk. He's *doing / making* a complaint about the restaurant.
f I can't *do / make* up my mind. Which should I buy? Red or green?
g We're *having / making* a wonderful holiday in Sicily.
h The children were very good and didn't *have / make* a fuss.

3 Complete the sentences with *have*, *make* or *do*. These expressions are not in the grammar information! First, guess the answers. Then use your dictionary to check.

a Right, children! Bedtime! Go and __do__ your teeth!
b Last night I saw a magician .... an amazing magic trick.
c You were very rude to Jude. Are you going to .... an apology?
d Did you hear the news? Philomena is going to .... a baby!
e Marty wants someone to .... her hair before the party.
f I think the President is going to .... a long speech.
g John wanted to stay but he didn't .... time.
h I tried to .... my best – and I passed the exam!
i Jess will be late. She .... a terrible headache.

4 INTERNET QUIZ

Search for the underlined word(s). Complete the first space with *have* or *make* in the correct form. Write a suitable noun in the second space.

a On 12 August 1908 a factory in Detroit __made__ the first Model T Ford __car__ .
b In 1928 Alexander Fleming .... a mistake with an experiment – and discovered ....!
c Fabergé .... beautiful .... with gold, silver and jewels.
d Rip Van Winkle .... a very long .... – for twenty years!
e On 21 July 1969 US President Richard Nixon .... a phone call to the ....
f Samuel Taylor Coleridge .... a strange dream in 1797. When he woke up, he wrote Kubla Khan – a very famous ....

More practice

> Auxiliary verbs are the 'little verbs' that go together with a 'main verb' to make different tenses.

Present Progressive

Present Simple

Past Simple

Present Perfect

Past Progressive

BE	
Present Progressive: '*m/am/'s/is/'re/are*	*She's working.*
Present Progressive questions: *am/is/are*	*Is he changing?*
Present Progressive negatives: *am not/isn't/aren't*	*We aren't trying.*
Past Progressive: *was/were*	*I was watching TV.*
Past Progressive questions: *was/were*	*Were you reading?*
Past Progressive negatives: *wasn't/weren't*	*They weren't listening.*

HAVE	
Present Perfect: '*ve/have/'s/has*	*I've been there.*
Present Perfect questions: *have/has*	*Have you finished?*
Present Perfect negatives: *haven't/hasn't*	*It hasn't worked.*

DO	
Present Simple questions: *do/does*	*Do you like butter?*
Present Simple negatives: *don't/doesn't*	*They don't play football.*
Past Simple questions: *did*	*Did he finish the job?*
Past Simple negatives: *didn't*	*I didn't go.*

1 Complete the sentences with *does*, *has* or *is*.

a _____Has_____ he given you a copy of the handout?

b What _____does_____ your cat like to eat?

c Why .... this train moving so slowly?

d .... the sun shine into this room?

e .... the sun shining outside?

f What .... happening in the square?

g .... Kirsty watched this DVD yet?

h Where .... Sanjeev hide his printer paper?

i Where .... Sanjeev hidden his printer paper?

j Where .... Sanjeev hiding his printer paper?

2 Does *'s* mean *has* or *is*?

a Margaret's never been to Singapore. _____has_____

b She's walking beside the sea. _____is_____

c Our teacher's shown us the answers. ....

d Our teacher's showing us the answers. ....

e Where's your grandfather going? ....

f The cat's finished the milk. ....

g Mike's gone swimming. ....

3 Complete the sentences with *don't*, *doesn't*, *haven't*, *hasn't*, *aren't* or *isn't*.

a Michael _____isn't_____ staying at this hotel.

b Shari .... like pop music.

c The teacher .... marking our essays today.

d Tom .... written an email to his dad yet.

e The football players .... finished their match.

f You can go the show if you want to. We .... going.

g I .... want to complain, but this coffee is cold.

h You .... enjoying the show. Let's go home.

4 Complete the questions with *Did*, *Was* or *Were*.

a _____Was_____ the cat eating its lunch?

b .... you meet anyone at the gym?

c .... someone steal my biscuit?

d .... the athletes running or resting?

e .... you hear the news?

f .... the alarm ringing when you went into the office?

g .... the children go swimming today?

5 THE (TOUGH) ONE

Think about the meaning of the sentences and answer the questions.

a 'My hand's cold.' How many hands?

....

b 'My hands are cold.' How many hands?

....

c 'The cars arrived.' One car – or more than one?

....

d 'The car's arrived.' One car – or more than one?

....

e 'We're there.' Now – or in the past?

....

f 'We were there.' Now – or in the past?

....

g 'We have one.' Is *have* an auxiliary verb or a main verb?

....

h 'We have won.' Is *have* an auxiliary verb or a main verb?

....

6 Which sentences in **5** do the pictures show?

1

Sentence h – 'We have won'

2

....

3

....

4

....

5

....

6

....

I can... Talk about things I like and dislike doing

love, like, enjoy, hate, etc. + infinitive/-ing • would like + infinitive

It's your birthday next week! What would you really, really, really like to do?

Well ... I love going on rollercoasters and fast rides so ... I'd like to go to a theme park ... Yes! I'd love to go to RetroWorld!

... but I hate going on long car journeys. I enjoy flying, though, so ... I want to go by plane ... but I can't stand waiting at airports.

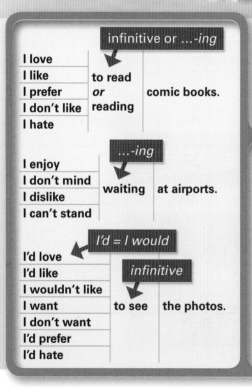

Actually ... I think ... I'd prefer to stay at home.

infinitive or ...-ing

I love		
I like	to read	
I prefer	*or*	comic books.
I don't like	reading	
I hate		

...-ing

I enjoy		
I don't mind		
I dislike	waiting	at airports.
I can't stand		

I'd = I would

infinitive

I'd love		
I'd like		
I wouldn't like		
I want	to see	the photos.
I don't want		
I'd prefer		
I'd hate		

Some verbs go with ...

to infinitive

They want <u>to go</u> soon. She'd like <u>to eat</u> dessert. We'd love <u>to escape</u> from here.

...-ing form

He really dislikes <u>cooking</u>. I enjoy <u>laughing</u> at a good film. I don't mind <u>staying</u> here.

either *to infinitive* or -...ing

She loves <u>making</u> pies. She loves <u>to make</u> pies. I hate <u>to be</u> late. I hate <u>being</u> late.

SAME meaning!

1 Underline the correct word. (Sometimes both words are correct!)

a Dominic would like <u>to go</u> / going to the market tonight.

b The children want *to watch* / *watching* a cartoon film.

c Our friends always love *to visit* / *visiting* your country cottage.

d I can't stand *to go* / *going* to the dentist.

e I prefer *to have* / *having* my hair long.

f I'd hate *to see* / *seeing* my old toys again.

g I like *to listen* / *listening* to classical music.

2 Put the verbs in brackets in the correct form: *to* infinitive or *-ing*. (Sometimes both words are correct!)

a I'd like ....to say.... (say) something about our new manager.

b We'd like .... (buy) some souvenirs.

c The Smiths always enjoy .... (go) on holiday to Croatia.

d Martha hates .... (eat) broccoli!

e I can't stand .... (hear) mice behind the walls of my room!

f Kieran loves .... (stay) at home with a pizza and a good film.

More practice

I can ... Talk about things I was able to do in the past (93)

could

> I'm watching a French film now and I can understand it!

`present`

> We can't swim this month because they're rebuilding the swimming pool.

> I watched an English film last night and I could understand it!

`past`

> We couldn't swim last month because I hurt my leg.

---

can = it is possible for me now
could = it was possible for me in the past
I couldn't afford it. = I didn't have enough money to buy it.

Questions

Could	you	understand the language	when	you	lived in Saudi Arabia?
	he/she	cook well		he/she	was/were young?
	they	use the machine		they	worked there?

Short answers

Yes,	you	could.	No,	you	couldn't.
	he/she			he/she	
	they			they	

---

1 Make *I couldn't ...* answers for the questions. Use the words in the box.

> answer any of the questions
> find my glasses
> ~~remember the room number~~
> sleep last night   start the car
> understand the announcements

a Why were you late for the meeting?
I couldn't remember the room number.

b Why do you look so tired?

c Why were you looking under the chairs?

d Why did you get on the wrong train?

e Why didn't you pass your driving test?

f Why did you leave the exam after only ten minutes?

2 Tom is 40 today! Complete his sentences with your own ideas.

a I can't play any musical instruments now. But when I was 18, I could *play the guitar.*

b I can drive large buses and trucks. But when I was 18, I couldn't *drive a car or ride a motorbike!*

c I can't speak any foreign languages. But when I was 18, I could _____ .

d I can't ski or skate or do any exciting sports. But when I was 18, I could _____ .

e I can cook Italian food really well. But when I was 18, I couldn't _____ .

f I can design a great website. But when I was 18, I couldn't _____ .

g I can't stay in bed after 6.30! But when I was 18, I could _____ .

h I can make lots of money now. But when I was 18, I couldn't _____ .

More practice

I can ... Say that something is really important to do

must

I must lose weight this year.

I really must stop smoking.

I must call Anna before 9 o'clock.

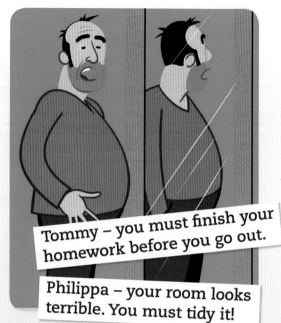

Tommy – you must finish your homework before you go out.

Philippa – your room looks terrible. You must tidy it!

I/you/he/she/it/we/they	must	do more exercise.
		drive on the right.
		leave the building.
		eat less fatty food.
		give Joan the instruction book.

Use *must* for ...

laws	rules	things we think are important or necessary to do	advice, suggestions, recommendations
All passengers must wear a seat belt.	*All students must be in school by 8.50.*	*I must tell Johnnie about the new album.*	*You must try this amazing new restaurant.*
You must have a full driving licence.	*You must write in black ink.*	*I'm so thirsty. I must get a drink before we leave.*	*You must meet Richard! He's great!*

Use *mustn't* when it is important that you do not do something.

You mustn't go into that room.

She mustn't tell Rachel.

The cook mustn't use peanuts.

They mustn't be late.

We mustn't ever forget him.

Really

In conversations use *really* to make your listener understand that what you are saying is true and important.

I really must go.

You really must try it.

1 Look at the notices. What must you do? Use a verb from A and words from B.

A	B
be	a seat belt
drive	~~safety glasses~~
lock	tall
~~put on~~	the door
show	very slowly
take off	your hands
wash	your helmet
wear	your passport

a

You must put on
safety glasses.

b

....

c

....

d

....

e

....

f

....

g

....

h

....

2 Say what you think you must do. Use *I must* and the verbs in the box (and more words if necessary).

call   eat   finish   ~~tell~~   update

a You hear a very funny joke. You know that your mum will enjoy it.
I must tell my mum.

b You promised to phone Harry before midday. You look at your watch. It's 11.55.
....

c You need to write two more pages in your essay before tomorrow. You have been playing games all evening.
....

d You are very hungry.
....

e You promised your friends that you'd put something new on your Facebook page. You haven't done it.
....

3 Tell small children what they *mustn't* do. Use the verbs in the box.

disturb   press   run   tell
~~touch~~   wake up   worry

a John-Paul is lifting his hand up to a valuable painting in an art gallery.
You mustn't touch the painting!

b Marilyn is shouting. The baby is asleep.
....

c Orlando is going to touch a button. He will turn the microwave on!
....

d Susie and Freda are chasing each other near the swimming pool. It's very slippery!
....

e Kelly wants to open the door of her father's room. He is working and needs to concentrate.
....

f Maisie is crying because she thinks her brother is very ill. But it's only a cold!
....

g Teresa's father shows her a lovely present for her mother. He says it's a secret until her birthday.
....

More practice

I can ...

Listen to other people's advice

should/must

You should go to university.

I think you should say 'no'.

You should come home more often.

You should say 'yes'.

You mustn't change your hairstyle.

You must get married soon.

You must study harder.

I don't think you should buy an apartment.

You mustn't eat so many chips.

You must save some money.

You must talk to him as soon as possible.

I think you should get a job.

You shouldn't smoke.

You shouldn't go on a diet.

You must think about it.

You should be careful.

You should make up your own mind!

People use *should* and *must* to tell you what they think is a good idea for you.

You should get a job and *You must get a job* both mean '*I believe it is a good idea for you to get a job.*'
Must is a little stronger than *should*.

I don't think you should go to Milan. = *I think you shouldn't go to Milan.* = '*I think it is not a good idea for you to go to Milan.*'

NB *I don't think* + positive = *I think* + negative

You	should must	visit	me soon.
		tell	your teacher.
		go	there now.
		meet	my parents.

You	shouldn't mustn't	buy	that new phone.
		be	late.
		talk	to her.
		play	so many computer games.

Ask for advice with *Should I ...?* or *Do you think I should ...?*

Should I change my hairstyle?

Should I go to the party?

Do you think I should give up smoking?

You can ask for general advice with *What should I do?*

1 Match the problems with the advice.

Problems

a I'm really overweight!

b I don't know what a spanner is!

c I want to know where she bought those wonderful headphones.

d I've lost my dictionary.

e I've always wanted to see China.

f All my friends have moved away.

g This food looks horrible.

h I'm feeling very ill.

Advice

1 You should look it up in an online dictionary.

2 You must go there next year.

3 You should go on a diet.

4 You must ask her.

5 You should join a club and meet some new people.

6 You should try it! It's delicious!

7 You must see a doctor as soon as possible.

8 You should get a new one.

2 Give advice to these people.

a Wendy works very late every day. She leaves the office at 9.30 p.m. When she gets home, she stays up until after 2 a.m. watching TV. She only sleeps for four hours. She is always very tired. At work, she drinks five or six large cups of coffee every day and eats badly – mainly snacks and chocolates.

You should *leave the office early* .

You should *eat better food* .

You should ....

You should ....

You shouldn't ....

b Tom has an important chemistry exam next week. He goes out every night and dances until midnight. He hasn't done any work for the exam. His books are in his bag at home. He hasn't opened them for two months!

You should ....

You should ....

You shouldn't ....

c Magda owns a very expensive car. She drives it very badly. She never puts on her seat belt. She eats burgers while she is driving. When she parks the car, she never locks the door! She doesn't have any insurance.

You shouldn't ....

You shouldn't ....

You should ....

3 Make questions to ask for advice with *Should I ... ?* Use the verbs in brackets.

a My clothes are very old. (buy)
Should I buy some new clothes?

b My girlfriend hasn't phoned me for a week. (call)
....

c I'm 18! I don't want to live at home with my parents any more. (leave)
....

d My hair is brown. I want to be blonde! (dye)
....

e I lent my friend $20. He hasn't mentioned it for weeks. (remind)
....

f I lent my friend $20. He hasn't mentioned it for weeks. (forget about)
....

g Someone told me a secret. I think it's important for Nick to hear it. (tell)
....

4 Give advice. Use *I think you should* ... (Different answers may be possible.)

a

I think you should
comb your hair.

b

....

c

....

d

....

e

....

f

....

I can ... Say how people and things are different

-er comparatives

Age: 276
Height: 1.6 metres
Cleverness: 170
Health: 39
Kindness: 78
Strength: 12

Age: 46
Height: 2.2 metres
Cleverness: 4
Health: 49
Kindness: 9
Strength: 92

Age: 37
Height: 1.9 metres
Cleverness: 82
Health: 39
Kindness: 17
Strength: 85

Age: 107
Height: 1.7 metres
Cleverness: 95
Health: 87
Kindness: 74
Strength: 56

The elf is older than the thief.

The thief is healthier than the wizard.

The troll is taller than the thief.

The wizard is much cleverer than the troll.

The thief is much stronger than the wizard.

adjective + *er*:	tall→taller slow→slower old→older
ending in *e + r*:	nice→nicer brave→braver
double consonant:	fat→fatter thin→thinner slim→slimmer
y → *ier*.	happy→happier funny→funnier noisy→noisier
irregular:	good→better bad→worse

Use *much* if you think there is a big difference:

Fred's taller than John.

Sam's much taller than Anna.

My brother			older		Leo.
Clara			younger		Sonia.
The wizard			fitter		your boss.
Our teacher	's	(much)	thinner	than	the elf.
That girl			shorter		you.
The robot			taller		my father.
This elephant			healthier		that musician.

1 Write the comparatives.

  a fast   *faster*

  b sad

  c easy

  d large

  e pretty

  f big

  g good

  h wise

  i lovely

  j bad

  k wet

2 Look at the cards again. Make true sentences.

  a (old / troll / elf)

    The elf's older than the troll.

  b (tall / wizard / thief)

  c (young / wizard / thief)

  d (kind / wizard / troll)

  e (strong / elf / thief)

  f (weak / wizard / thief)

  g (short / wizard / elf)

  h (healthy / elf / troll)

  i (clever / thief / elf)

3 What is the opposite of these words?

  a taller   *shorter*

  b fatter

  c stronger

  d faster

  e noisier

  f heavier

  g better

4 ABOUT YOU

Make true sentences about people in your family.

  a (young) *My sister is younger than me.*

  b (old)

  c (tall)

  d (fit)

  e (noisy)

  f (heavy)

5 INTERNET QUIZ

Write comparisons of these things. Use the words in brackets.

  a Yangtze River; Yellow River (long)

    The Yangtze River is longer than the Yellow River.

  b The Taj Mahal; Great Pyramid at Ghiza (old)

  c The Shard in London; Taipei 101 (tall)

  d Sahara desert; Karakum desert (hot)

  e Sahara desert; Karakum desert (big)

  f Sahara desert; Karakum desert (rainy)

Compare books, films and other things

Comparatives with **more** and **less**

This perfume is more expensive than that one.

Archie McAndrews is less popular than Phil Grady.

Ben's book is more interesting than Alex's.

I think *Shark Bite 3D* will be more exciting than *People Talking*!

Yes! You're right. That film looks much more boring!

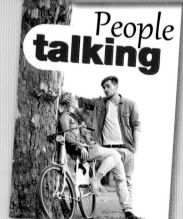

Short words make comparatives with *-er*:
bright → brighter wide → wider tasty → tastier big → bigger

Longer words make comparatives with *more* and *less*:
important → more important / less important
serious → more serious / less serious

more = +   **less = −**

Some two-syllable words can use either *-er* or *more/less*:
friendly → friendlier <u>or</u> more friendly
handsome → handsomer <u>or</u> more handsome
polite → politer <u>or</u> more polite

NB fun → ~~funner~~ → more fun / less fun

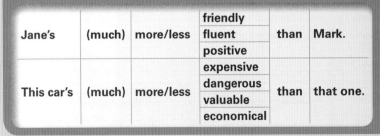

Jane's	(much)	more/less	friendly	than	Mark.
			fluent		
			positive		
This car's	(much)	more/less	expensive	than	that one.
			dangerous		
			valuable		
			economical		

If you say something is *more likely* than something else, you mean there is more chance of it happening.
I think Jack's more likely to win than Ryan.

1 Make comparatives with either *-er* or *more*.

a cold   *colder*

b interesting   *more interesting*

c successful   ....

d light   ....

e modern   ....

f delicious   ....

g simple   ....

h comfortable   ....

i popular   ....

j windy   ....

k relaxed   ....

l hot   ....

m confident   ....

2 Write comparisons with *more* or *less*. Use the words in brackets.

a 'There are too many people in this café! Let's go to Giuseppe's.'
'Good idea! That'll probably be ....*less crowded*....!' (crowded)

b 'Which smartphone should I get?'
'Well, they're both good. This one is fantastic – but it's .... , I'm afraid.' (expensive)

c 'Was the hotel alright?'
'No! It was much .... than the one in Belgrade!' (comfortable)

d 'Don't drop the plates this time!'
'OK! I promise I'll be ....' (careful)

e 'I'm afraid that buses only stop here twice a day.'
'Oh dear! That's much .... than in my town.' (frequent)

f 'Why are you handwriting a letter instead of sending an email?'
'I want to make it ....' (personal)

g 'This Damien Hirst sculpture is worth thousands of pounds.'
'Yes – but that Van Gogh is much .... It's worth millions!' (valuable)

3 Make comparative sentences. Use comparative forms of the adjectives in the box.

> active comfortable detailed difficult
> ~~experienced~~ likely modern popular

a Ursula has worked here for 20 years. Phil has worked here for four years.
Ursula is more experienced than Phil.

b The red chair is hard and lumpy. The sofa isn't hard or lumpy.
The red chair is ....

c Most students could answer Question 7. Only two students could answer Question 8.
Question 8 was ....

d The Cottonly Centre was built in 2010 and has lots of new features. The Arnold Centre was built in 1984 and is quite old-fashioned now.
The Arnold Centre is ....

e Sue will probably pass the exam. Hal will probably fail.
Hal's ....

f Martin goes to the gym on Tuesdays. Penny jogs every day and plays tennis twice a week.
Martin is ....

g Leo's new song *My Tiger* has sold thousands. No one bought his last song *Rainy Fields*.
My Tiger is ....

h The maps in the white book only show a few main roads and buildings. The maps in the red book have all the roads and every building.
The maps in the white book are ....

4 It's the year 2125. **B** thinks his house robot is not as good as **A**'s. Complete his sentences.

a *My robot is less intelligent than yours.* (intelligent)

b .... (slow)

c .... (efficient)

d .... (expensive)

e .... (heavy)

f .... (annoying)

g ....
.... (very likely to go wrong)

More practice

Real travellers review hotels ...

Pushkin Hotel
***

8,000 roubles

suburbs

32 bedrooms

Traveller reviews
'Great value for money' '... quite clean – but not perfect' 'fantastic breakfast' 'rude staff'

Metropole Hotel
*****

13,500 roubles

2 minutes' walk to the town centre

231 bedrooms

Traveller reviews
'... very expensive. Not worth it!' 'very clean and tidy' 'Breakfast is OK. Nothing special' 'Staff are very helpful'

Chaika Hotel
**

6,800 roubles

1 km to the town centre

7 bedrooms

Traveller reviews
'Even 5,000 roubles would be too much!' 'horrible dirty rooms!' 'Breakfast is just bread and jam' 'Staff smile but can't help much.'

The Pushkin has more stars than the Chaika, but ... **the Metropole has the most stars.**

◄ *the most/least + noun* ►

The Pushkin has fewer stars than the Metropole, but ... **the Chaika has the least stars.**

The Pushkin's more expensive than the Chaika, but ... **the Metropole's the most expensive.**

◄ *the most/least + adjective* ►

The Pushkin is less expensive than the Metropole, but ... **the Chaika's the least expensive.**

The Chaika isn't close to the town centre. The Pushkin is closer, but ... **the Metropole's the closest.**

Short adjectives

	adjective	comparative	superlative	
+ -est:	tall	taller	the tallest	She's the tallest.
double consonant:	big	bigger	the biggest	It's the biggest.
ending in –y:	happy	happier	the happiest	He's the happiest.
ending in -e:	nice	nicer	the nicest	This one is the nicest.
irregular:	good	better	the best	This is the best hotel.
	bad	worse	the worst	That's the worst café.

Long adjectives

	adjective	comparative	superlative	
+ most:	expensive	more expensive	the most expensive	It's the most expensive.
+ least:	interesting	less interesting	the least interesting	It's the least interesting.

When we compare two things, we use a comparative:

 Fred is taller than John.

When we compare one thing with two or more other things, we can use a superlative:

 Fred is taller than John and Sam. He's the tallest.

1 Make superlatives with either *the -est* or *the most*.

a exciting *the most exciting*
b small *the smallest*
c loud ....
d enjoyable ....
e tidy ....
f delicious ....
g lovely ....
h wide ....
i beautiful ....

2 Look at the hotel information again. Answer the questions.

a Which hotel is the cheapest? *The Chaika*
b Which hotel is the furthest from the town centre? ....
c Which hotel has the smallest number of bedrooms? ....
d Which hotel has the worst breakfast? ....
e Which hotel is the dirtiest? ....
f Which hotel has the most helpful staff? ....
g Which hotel is the best value for money? ....

3 **ABOUT** **YOU**

Write sentences about people, places and things you know.

a *My uncle Leopold is the* tallest *person in my family.*
b *The shop assistants at the Grand are the* least helpful *in town.*
c .... most annoying
d .... best
e .... least interesting
f .... most humorous
g .... most enjoyable
h .... worst

4 **INTERNET** **QUIZ** 🔍

Answer each question with a superlative. Use adjectives from the box.

> dangerous ~~high~~ large
> long old valuable

a Everest is *the highest* mountain in the world.
b The Brazilian Wandering Spider is .... spider in the world.
c The Nile is .... river in the world.
d Oxford is .... university in England.
e Jupiter is .... planet in the solar system.
f *The Scream* is .... painting by Edward Munch.

Present Simple jokes

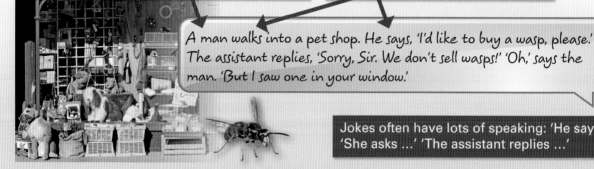

> Jokes often start like this: 'Someone walks in somewhere ...'

> The story is about the past – but the speaker uses Present Simple!

> A man walks into a pet shop. He says, 'I'd like to buy a wasp, please.' The assistant replies, 'Sorry, Sir. We don't sell wasps!' 'Oh,' says the man. 'But I saw one in your window.'

> Jokes often have lots of speaking: 'He says ..' 'She asks ...' 'The assistant replies ...'

> A man walks into a shop and says 'Can I have a pack of helicopter flavour potato chips?' The assistant says 'Sorry. We've only got plain.'

> English jokes often use **puns**. A pun is a word that has the same sound as another word – but a different meaning.

> **Plain** potato chips are chips without an added flavour. **Plane** is short for aeroplane – a vehicle that can fly.

1 Match the beginnings and ends of the jokes.

a A man walks into a bookshop. He says, 'Can I have a book by Shakespeare?' The assistant replies, 'Certainly, Sir. Which one?' The man says ...

b A man walks into a station ticket office. He says, 'Can I have a return ticket, please?' The assistant asks, 'Where to?' The man replies ...

c A man gets onto a bus. He asks the driver, 'Does this bus go to the hospital?' The driver replies ...

d A man walks into the doctor's room. 'Ah, hello!' says the doctor. 'I haven't seen you for a long time!' 'I know,' says the man ...

e A skeleton walks into a party. Another guest says, 'Hello. Are you on your own?' 'Yes,' says the skeleton ...

f A man and a zebra walk into a café. They eat a big meal. The zebra lies down and falls asleep on the café floor. The café owner comes over to the man and says 'You can't leave that lying there.' The man replies ...

g Two fried eggs and a piece of toast walk into a café. 'Sorry,' says the owner...

h A man walks into a fish shop with a large fish under his arm. He says 'Do you make fishcakes?' The assistant replies 'Yes, of course.' 'Good,' says the man ...

i Two lions are walking in Trafalgar Square in London. One lion turns to the other and says ...

1 'It's his birthday.'
2 'I've been very ill.'
3 'William.'
4 'I had no body to go with.'
5 'We don't serve breakfast.'
6 'It's very empty today, isn't it?'
7 'Only when it's ill!'
8 'It's not a lion. It's a zebra.'
9 'Well ... back to here, of course!'

2 Here is a longer joke. Complete it with the verbs in the box.

> asks bites doesn't opens replies said screams sits ~~walks~~

A man ___walks___ ^a into a café. He _____ ^b down next to a woman and a dog. The man _____ ^c the woman, 'Does your dog bite?' 'No,' _____ ^d the woman. Suddenly the dog _____ ^e his mouth and _____ ^f the man. The man _____ ^g and then says, 'You _____ ^h your dog doesn't bite!' 'He _____ ^i,' says the woman. 'That's not my dog.'

3 Choose your favourite joke from this page and try to remember it. Practise saying it from memory. Tell other people.

More practice

Irregular verbs

Infinitive	Past Simple	Past participle
be	was / were	been
become	became	become
begin	began	begun
blow	blew	blown
break	broke	broken
bring	brought	brought
build	built	built
burn	burnt / burned	burnt / burned
buy	bought	bought
catch	caught	caught
choose	chose	chosen
come	came	come
cost	cost	cost
creep	crept	crept
cut	cut	cut
dig	dug	dug
do	did	done
draw	drew	drawn
drink	drank	drunk
drive	drove	driven
eat	ate	eaten
fall	fell	fallen
feel	felt	felt
fight	fought	fought
find	found	found
fly	flew	flown
forget	forgot	forgotten
freeze	froze	frozen
get	got	got
give	gave	given
go	went	gone / been
grow	grew	grown
have	had	had
hear	heard	heard
hide	hid	hidden
hit	hit	hit
keep	kept	kept
know	knew	known
lay	laid	laid

Infinitive	Past Simple	Past participle
lead	led	led
learn	learnt / learned	learnt / learned
leave	left	left
let	let	let
lose	lost	lost
make	made	made
meet	met	met
put	put	put
read	read	read
ride	rode	ridden
ring	rang	rung
rise	rose	risen
run	ran	run
say	said	said
see	saw	seen
sell	sold	sold
send	sent	sent
show	showed	shown
shut	shut	shut
sing	sang	sung
sit	sat	sat
sleep	slept	slept
smell	smelt	smelt
speak	spoke	spoken
spend	spent	spent
stand	stood	stood
steal	stole	stolen
swim	swam	swum
take	took	taken
teach	taught	taught
tear	tore	torn
tell	told	told
think	thought	thought
throw	threw	thrown
understand	understood	understood
wake	woke	woken
wear	wore	worn
win	won	won
write	wrote	written

Answer key

(1) I can ... Describe things

1 [Possible answers]
  b It's tall. **c** It's broken. **d** It's small. **e** It's far away.
  f It's long.

2 [Possible answers]
  b It's tall. It's beautiful.
  c It's long. It's far away.
  d It's big. It's beautiful. It's far away.
  e It's huge. It's far away.
  f It's big. It's beautiful. It's far away.
  g It's small. It's near.

(2) I can ... Talk about the weather and time

1 **b** It's a quarter to eight. **c** It's two thirty five.
  d It's a quarter past eight. **e** It's half past one.

2 **b** It's **c** to **d** rainy **e** half

3 Students' own answers.

(3) I can ... Introduce myself and other people

1 **b** 5 **c** 1 **d** 2 **e** 4

2 **b** 're/are **c** 's/is **d** are **e** 's/is, 'm/am **f** 's/is

3 **b** she's **c** You're **d** They're **e** We're

4 Students' own answers.

(4) I can ... Say how people feel

1 **b** I'm tired. **c** I'm cold. **d** I'm happy.
  e I'm frightened. **f** I'm bored.

2 **b** 's **c** are **d** 's **e** are **f** 's **g** 's **h** are **i** is

3 [Possible answers]
  b I'm tired. **c** I'm excited. **d** I'm worried.
  e I'm happy / excited.

(5) I can ... Say where things are (1)

1 **b** at, in **c** on, at **d** in, on **e** at, on **f** on

2 **b** It's in room 2B. **c** It's in the cupboard.
  d It's on the third floor. **e** It's at the doctor's.
  f It's on the train.

(6) I can ... Say what is <u>not</u> true

1 **b** 5 **c** 2 **d** 6 **e** 3 **f** 1

2 **b** This film isn't boring.
  c I'm not very hungry.
  d We aren't late.
  e Mark isn't a doctor.
  f I'm not surprised about it.
  g Her story isn't true.
  h It isn't very rainy today.
  i They aren't from Sri Lanka.

3 Students' own answers.
  a is/isn't **b** is/isn't **c** are/aren't
  d are/aren't **e** is/isn't **f** are/aren't

(7) I can ... Ask about people's lives (1)

1 **b** Are **c** Are **d** Is **e** Am **f** Is **g** Are

2 **b** Is the train late?
  c Are the clothes dry?
  d Is the printer on?
  e Are the children in the library?
  f Are you happy with your work?
  g Are you sorry?

(8) I can ... Give short answers

1 **b** 1 **c** 5 **d** 4 **e** 7 **f** 2 **g** 6

2 **b** Yes, she is. **c** No, it isn't. **d** No, they aren't. **e** No, it isn't.
  f Yes, it is. **g** No, he isn't. **h** Yes, they are. **i** Yes, he is.
  j Yes, they are.

3 Students' own answers.

4 Students' own answers.

(9) I can ... Ask about people's lives (2)

1 **b** 7 **c** 1 **d** 2 **e** 3 **f** 4 **g** 6

2 **b** How old **c** Are you **d** Why are you
  e When is **f** What are **g** Why's

3 **b** Where **c** How **d** When / What
  e How **f** Why **g** Where / What **h** How

4 [Possible answers]
  How are you?
  How is your brother?
  How much are the sandwiches?
  How much is the book?
  What is the answer?
  What is your name?
  Where are your sandwiches?
  Where is your brother?
  Why are you tired?

(10) I can ... Say what is in a place

1 **b** There's **c** There are **d** There's
  e There are **f** There are

2 **b** Is there **c** Are there **d** Is there **e** Is there

3 **b** Yes, there is. **c** Yes, there are. **d** No, there aren't.

4 **a** There are 31,536,000 seconds in an ordinary year.
  b There are 42 dots on a pair of dice.
  c There aren't any penguins near the North Pole.

(11) I can ... Talk about friends and relations

1 **b** his **c** my, our, their **d** our **e** my, her **f** his
  g our

2 **b** their **c** her **d** my / our **e** our **f** your **g** Their
  h his

3 **b** my homework **c** its economy **d** his shoes
  e her boyfriend **f** their lunch **g** our favourite

(12) I can ... Talk about things I have

1 Students' own answers.

2 **b** I've got a large house.
  c I've got a new phone.
  d Jane has got blue eyes.
  e The students have got As.
  f Juan has got a problem.

3 Students' own answers.

(13) I can ... Talk about my health

1 **b** 've **c** 's **d** have **e** 've

2 **a** 3 **b** 6 **c** 4 **d** 1 **e** 5

3 2 She's got a cough.
  7 He's got a toothache.

4 Students' own answers.

(14) I can ... Ask if people have things

1 **b** Does she have the correct answer?
  c Have you got a moment?
  d Have we got everything?
  e Does he have brown eyes or blue eyes?
  f Do you have a suggestion?

2 **b** have **c** Has **d** do **e** Does **f** you

3 **b** Do you have a dictionary?
c Has she got a dog?
d Do you have a credit card?
e Have you got a pen?
f Does she have a ticket?
g Do we have time?

(15) I can ... Give short answers about things I have

1 **b** it does **c** I have **d** I don't **e** they do
f we haven't **g** it doesn't **h** it has

2 **b** Yes, I have / No, I haven't.
c Yes, they have / No, they haven't.
d Yes, I do / No, I don't.
e Yes, it does / No, it doesn't.
f Yes, it does / No, it doesn't.
g Yes, I have / No, I haven't.
h Yes, it has / No, it hasn't.

(16) I can ... Talk about things I haven't got

1 **b** haven't got **c** hasn't got **d** haven't got
e hasn't got **f** haven't got

2 **b** doesn't **c** haven't **d** hasn't **e** don't **f** hasn't

3 **a** 4 **b** 2 **c** 1 **d** 3

4 **a** a tail **b** Venus, Mercury **c** hair

(17) I can ... Use _this, that, these, those_

1 **b** That's **c** That's **d** Those are **e** This is
f Those are **g** That's **h** These are **i** This is **j** This is

2 **b** That **c** This **d** Those **e** That **f** These

3 **b** This **c** that **d** That **e** That **f** this **g** That **h** That

(18) I can ... Say what I can do

1 Students' own answers.

2 [Possible answers]
c Can you use Photoshop? / PowerPoint?
d Can you play squash? / football?
e Can you read Spanish? / speak Spanish? /read Japanese?
f Can you say _yacht_? / Can you spell yacht?
g Can you play the piano? / guitar?
h Can you tweet? / Can you use Facebook?
i Can you repair a car? / drive a car?

3 [Possible answers]
I can / can't play the violin.
John can / can't do the homework.
She can / can't use spreadsheets.
My brother can / can't play snooker.
Sue can / can't do her homework.
They can / can't use spreadsheets.

(19) I can ... Ask people to help me

1 **b** 3 **c** 2 **d** 4 **e** 1

2 **b** Could you / Can you help me with my homework, please?
c Could you / Can you pass the tomato ketchup, please?
d Could you / Can you lend me some money, please?
e Could you / Can you show me that necklace, please?

(20) I can ... Ask for permission

1 **b** make **c** ask **d** call **e** have

2 **b** Can I / Could I look at your homework answers, please?
c Can I / Could I take the last chocolate, please?
d Can I / Could I check my emails on your computer, please?
e Can I / Could I come to work late tomorrow, please?

(21) I can ... Talk about habits, routines and repeated actions

1 **b** runs **c** catches **d** flies **e** does **f** talks
g fries **h** washes **i** finishes **j** takes
k cuts **l** copies **m** undoes **n** tries **o** drives

2 **b** talks **c** tests **d** unlocks **e** walks **f** watches

g tries **h** calls **i** says **j** closes **k** turns **l** goes

3 Students' own answers.

(22) I can ... Say how often things happen

1 **b** I am / I'm never home before 10 p.m.
c We hardly ever do our homework.
d You usually cry when you watch a romantic film!
e She is/ She's often at work before anyone else.
f They never make cakes for the school.
g He rarely eats vegetables.

2 Students' own answers.

(23) I can ... Talk about days when I do things

1 **b** on Sunday 19th / on the 19th / on 19th January
c on Christmas Day / on 25th December
d on Saturday morning(s)/ on Saturday 28th
e on Wednesdays
f on Tuesday afternoon, on Tuesday evening
g on Sundays
h on my birthday

2 Students' own answers.

(24) I can ... Talk about times when things happen

1 **b** at **c** on **d** at **e** at **f** In **g** at **h** in **i** in, at

2

on	in
on New Year's Day on Wednesday evening on the first day of January	in the evening in spring in March in 2001

at	no preposition
at 2 o'clock at lunchtime at night at half past twelve	yesterday this morning tonight

3 **b** 4 **c** 5 **d** 1 **e** 2

4 [Possible answers]
b Sunday **c** tonight / tomorrow **d** Wednesday(s)
e January **f** Independence **g** July **h** Monday
i midday **j** night **k** Monday

(25) I can ... Talk about things that are generally true

1 **b** love **c** cooks **d** uses **e** opens **f** close **g** write

2 **b** She lives in New York.
c She wears glasses.
d She drives to work.
e She loves ice cream.
f She works in a (fast food) diner.

3 **a** Arctic **b** 100° Celsius **c** the Sun **d** during the day
e eucalyptus leaves **f** their mate **g** feet

(26) I can ... Say what isn't true

1 **b** I don't like chocolate cake.
c She doesn't play football on Wednesdays.
d The new printer doesn't work very well.
e Martin doesn't sing blues songs.
f I don't visit my grandparents at the weekend.

2 **b** She doesn't like ice cream.
c They don't know the answer.
d They don't speak English.
e They don't / It doesn't open on Sundays.
f It doesn't work.

3 **b** The US President doesn't live in Downing Street. He/she lives in the White House.
c Water doesn't freeze at 50° Celsius. It freezes at 0° Celsius.
d Carrots don't grow on trees. They grow in the ground.

Answer key

e The sun doesn't rise in the north. It rises in the east.

f Mobile phones don't use wind power. They use battery power.

(27) I can ... Ask about habits and routines

1 b Do c Do d Does e Does f Do g Do
h Do i Do j Does

2 Students' own answers.

3 Students' own answers.

(28) I can ...Ask for more information about habits and routines

1 b 5 c 1 d 7 e 8 f 2 g 4 h 6

2 b do you work c does your company make
d do your customers like e do you go
f do you do g do you enjoy

(29) I can ... Say where things are (2)

1 B is in front of the school.
C is next to the school / between the school and the tree.
D is behind the school.
E is under the tree.
F is on top of the tree.
G is in the school.

2 b in front of c behind d next to e opposite
f in front of g between h behind

(30) I can ... Talk about what is happening now

1 b, d, e

2 b 's cooking. c 're laughing. d 's barking.
e 're talking f 's raining.

3 b 'm / am cooking c 's / is walking d are talking
e 'm / am wearing f 's / is playing

4 Students' own answers.

(31) I can ... Make ...ing endings correctly

1 b watching c using d writing e smoking
f cutting g building h baking i staying
j laughing k stopping l going

2 b chatting c taking d lying e heating f using g getting

(32) I can ... Avoid unnecessary repetition

1 b The children are singing, dancing and laughing.
c That's dangerous. You are running and eating at the same time!
d Wilga is doing her homework and playing a computer game!
e I'm sitting in my car and waiting for George.
f Hello! Can anyone hear me? I'm standing outside your front door, trying to get in and pressing all the buttons but the door doesn't open. Hello?

(33) I can ... Send messages about what I'm doing now

1 b I'm running to work. c I'm working at home.
d I'm robbing a bank. e I'm meeting a customer.
g I'm flying to Rio.

2 b We're / We **are** all listening to the radio news.
c I'm working on my computer. ✓
d I'm / **am** playing chess with my brother.
e Rasa and Elena is **are** working at home today
f The girl are **'s / is** singing a lovely song. / The girls are singing a lovely song.

(34) I can ... Write an email about my life now

1 [Possible answers]
b 'm listening c 's eating d 's growing
e 's staying f 's making

2 a 'm catching the train / 'm cycling/ 'm walking
b 's going c 're staying

3 b 'm sharing c are studying d 're taking
e 'm working f 'm failing g 'm saving

(35) I can ... Talk about planned future events

1 b F c N d F e F f F g N h F i F

2 b On Sunday afternoon he's playing football.
c On Monday morning he's meeting Thai visitors.
d On Tuesday morning he's flying to Rome.
e On Wednesday he's presenting the company's new products to the Italian team.
f On Thursday he's flying back.
g On Friday he's reporting to the CEO and the board.

3 Students' own answers.

(36) I can ... Make an excuse about why I can't do something

1 b 'm flying c 'm catching d 'm driving
e are working f 'm leaving g 'm teaching

2 Students' own answers.

(37) I can ... Make Present Progressive negatives and questions

1 b We aren't doing very well in the tests.
c The children aren't playing computer games.
d I'm not cooking supper again tonight.
e The engine isn't starting.
f It isn't snowing in Saudi Arabia!
g The teacher isn't waiting for Amir.

2 b Is Vicki meeting the visitors?
c Why are the children singing?
d Is our plane leaving soon?
e Am I pronouncing this word correctly?
f Where are the players going?
g Are you getting a new car?

(38) I can ... Remember which verbs aren't usually used in the Present Progressive

1 b I know c I'm enjoying d I believe e I'm telling
f I remember g I understand h tastes

2 b understands, is trying c remember, know
d hate, smells e is crying, wants f loves, think

(39) I can ... Decide whether to use Present Simple or Present Progressive

1 b N c G d N e G f N

2 b they're staying c I always go
d Mahmoud's writing e I usually write, I'm blogging
f He's studying, she's doing g Matteo's texting

3 a Yes, he does. b No, he isn't. c No, he doesn't.
d Yes, she is. e Yes, she does.
f No, she isn't. g Yes, he does.

4 a I'm writing (my book).
b I write books. / I'm a writer.
c (ii)

(40) I can ... Talk about the past with was and were

1 c were, was d are e were f was, was, were g was, Were

2 b He was at a meeting. c It was in Italy.
d I was in a traffic jam. e It was $39. f No, it was boring.

3 a Armstrong and Aldrin were b Ang Lee was
c was, Japan d was, 52 e Uruguay was

(41) I can ... Talk about things that happened in the past (1)

1 b coughed c waited d watched e signed
f tried g followed h tasted i jumped
j remembered k played l carried m saved
n fried o jogged p pushed q travelled

2 b watched c fried d jumped, followed
e tasted f signed g carried h remembered

3 a 9 b 8 c 4 d 2 e 10 g 3 h 7 I 5 J 6

130

I can ... Talk about things that happened in the past (2)

1 b flew **c** drove **d** drew **e** climbed **f** left
g went **h** turned **i** opened **j** spoke
k met **l** raced **m** read **n** wrote

2 a When he finished, he got into his car and drove to the club. He put the cake on the table and asked everyone to have some. When they tasted it, they all said that it was delicious.
b She swam for 30 minutes and then did exercises for another half an hour. After that she felt tired! She had a quick shower and changed into her work clothes. She went out and caught the bus to her office. She worked until 5 p.m. and then jogged all the way home! She ate a healthy supper, switched on the TV and watched the news. Not surprisingly, she fell asleep in the chair!

3 b put on **c** climbed **d** rode **e** left **f** went
g heard **h** got off **i** walked **j** felt **k** crept
l saw **m** was **n** stood **o** had **p** noticed
q said **r** told

4 b Rontgen <u>won</u> the Nobel Prize in 1901 for his discovery of X-rays.
c On 17th December 1903 Wilbur and Orville Wright <u>flew</u> for the first time.
d In 1815 Napoleon and Wellington <u>fought</u> the Battle of Waterloo.
e John F Kennedy <u>became</u> the President of the USA in 1961.
f Neil Armstrong <u>walked</u> on the Moon in 1969.
g 1n 1962 The Beatles <u>sang</u> on TV for the first time.
h The Aztecs <u>built</u> many pyramids in Central America between the fourteenth and sixteenth centuries.
i Thomas Stafford & Alexei Leonov <u>met</u> in space on July 15th 1975.

 I can ... Ask about the past

1 b Did Rita and Pepe paint the house?
c Did she go to Dubai?
d Did they have a nice lunch together?
e Did Rihanna sing all evening?
f Did he make a nice meal?

2 b watch **c** eat **d** go **e** buy **f** have

3 b 4 c 1 d 5 e 2

44 I can ... Ask *Wh-* questions about the past

1 b What did she see?
c What did he / she write?
d Who did he meet?
e What did they sing?
f Where did they go?
g What did she do?
h Why did he laugh?
i Which book did she take?
j How many cakes did they make?
k Why did they leave?

2 b When did it happen?
c Why did you have the box?
d How much money did it have?
e Who did you ask for help?
f Where did you look?
g How long did you search?
h Where did you find it?
i How did you find it?

3 a [Possible answers]
How long did the cake last?
What did you eat for supper?
What did your father cook?
Where did the magician meet your father?
Where did you go last night?
Where did your father go?
Who did you meet in Rome?

Who did you meet?
Why did the magician eat the cake?
How did the magician make a rabbit?
Why did the magician go to Rome?
b [Possible answer]
How long did the magician cook the rabbit for your father in Rome last night?

 I can ... Give short answers about the past

1 b Yes, she did. **c** No, he didn't. **d** Yes, he did.
e No, he didn't. **f** Yes, it did. **g** No, she didn't.

2 Students' own answers.

46 I can ... Say what didn't happen in the past

1 b saw, didn't see **c** went, didn't go
d broke, didn't break **e** told, didn't tell

2 b He didn't listen to the radio.
c He didn't park on the street.
d He didn't run to the café.
e He didn't talk to his boss.
f He didn't feel sad.

47 I can ... Say what order things happened in

1 c X **d** X **e** Y **f** X **g** X

2 b before **c** before **d** After **e** After **f** before
g after

3 b When the bus stopped, Susie got off.
c When I lost my job in England, I moved to Canada.
d When they heard the alarm, the police rushed to the bank. / When the police heard the alarm, they rushed to the bank.
e When the car made a loud noise, the baby woke up.
f When I got your email, I tried to phone you.

48 I can ... Say when things happened

1 b the day before yesterday
c last year
d last night
e last weekend
f yesterday afternoon/evening

2 Students' own answers.

49 I can ... Say how long before now something happened

1 b The train left five minutes ago.
c Sharon passed her exam a year ago.
d Patrick phoned Dexter an hour and a half ago.
e I moved to Denver nine months ago.
f Sheila first heard this song two weeks ago.
g Shakespeare died about four hundred years ago.
h My uncle gave me this toy car 82 years ago.

2 Students' own answers.

50 I can ... Describe a journey

1 b 6 **c** 1 **d** 5 **e** 2 **f** 4

2 b into **c** through **d** along **e** around **f** over
g along

51 I can ... Make longer sentences

1 b I went to the petrol station and bought some flowers.
c Carrie turned the TV on and watched the news.
d Dan came to the meeting late and yawned all the time.
e Monty rang the doorbell and Lara opened the door.
f I arrived at 9.00 and went straight to Reception.

2 b Tony phoned his girlfriend three times but no one answered.
c Eva won the race but she didn't win a medal.
d Maria ate a lot of paella but she didn't have dessert.
e The music was wonderful but it was too loud.
f I failed my exam but it doesn't matter.

Answer key

3 c I went to the hairdresser's yesterday but they didn't have any space for me.
 d I went to the hairdresser's yesterday and had a great cut.
 e We apologised for our noisy party and gave them some flowers.
 f We apologised for our noisy party but they were still angry.
 g We were lost in the desert near Riyadh and didn't have much water.
 h We were lost in the desert but we had a lot of water.

52 I can ... Talk about reasons and results

1 b because c so d so e Because f because
 g so h so
2 b It was very late so Mike didn't phone Cindy.
 c Mike didn't feel very well so he didn't go to work.
 d Mike recommended Mahler's 2nd Symphony so Cindy listened to it today.
 e Mike bought some beautiful blue earrings for Cindy because he liked them.
 f The bus was full so Mike didn't get on it.

53 I can ... Tell a story about the past

1 b caught c broke d got e walked f got
 g didn't move h sat i announced j opened
 k ran l took m arrived n realised
 o didn't have p knocked
2 Possible answers
 b First, I caught the tram ...
 c Unfortunately, it broke down ...
 d Then I got off and walked.
3 Students' own answers.

54 I can ... Use the Past Simple

1 c What did you eat for lunch?
 d Why did you go on a diet?
 e What did you buy at the shops?
 f How much did your new mobile phone cost?
 g Did you sing at the party?
 h When did you get home last night?
 i Did you tell your parents about the show?
 j Why did you phone me?
2 b Did you check c I checked d Did he like
 e he cried f He didn't enjoy g did you do
 h I sang i Did you give j I forgot
 k I didn't give
3 c felt d told e didn't do f went g didn't work
 h learnt i designed j used k didn't think
 l bought m became n said o didn't like
4 b Why did you go?
 c How much did it cost?
 d What did you say?
 e Did you forget?
 f Did you cook it?

55 I can ... Ask about people's life experiences

1 b Have you ever painted a house?
 c Have you ever danced on a beach at night?
 d Have you ever cooked Indian food?
 e Have you ever played *Final Fantasy*?
 f Have you ever called the wrong phone number?
 g Have you ever talked for more than an hour on the phone?
 h Have you ever walked to work or school?
2 Students' own answers.

56 I can ... Make past participles

1 b Have you ever sung opera?
 c Have you ever ridden a motorbike?
 d Have you ever caught a cold?
 e Have you ever told a lie?
 f Have you ever kept chickens?

2 climb collect
3 b driven c heard d eaten e climbed
 f run g swum h flown i collected j lost
4

1	2	3
become	became	became
blow	blew	blown
begin	began	begun
catch	caught	caught
come	came	come
choose	chose	chosen
draw	drew	drawn
feel	felt	felt
find	found	found
freeze	froze	frozen
give	gave	given
know	knew	known
leave	left	left
make	made	made
say	said	said
speak	spoke	spoken
take	took	taken
win	won	won
write	wrote	written

5 b Have you ever sung in a karaoke bar?
 c Have you ever left a film before the end?
 d Have you ever forgotten someone's birthday?
 e Have you ever broken your leg?
 f Have you ever ridden a horse?
 g Have you ever seen a ghost?
 h Have you ever been on holiday on your own?
6 b Have you ever met a famous person? Yes, I have / No, I haven't.
 c Have you ever eaten a full English breakfast? Yes, I have / No, I haven't.
 d Have you ever seen a penguin? Yes, I have / No, I haven't.
 e Have you ever won a big prize? Yes, I have / No, I haven't.
 f Have you ever driven a truck? Yes, I have / No, I haven't.

57 I can ... Talk about experiences I have never had

1 b I've never seen a crocodile.
 c Jamie has never heard of dinosaurs.
 d Mrs Edwards has never taught this class.
 e Tom has never led a meeting before.
 f Suzy has never forgotten her first pop concert.
 g Sylvia has never woken up before eight o'clock.
2 Students' own answers.
3 Students' own answers.
4 [Possible answers]
 c 's never swum in the Pacific.
 d 's never owned a motorbike.
 e 's never worked in Australia.
 f 've never listened to jazz.
5 [Possible answers]
 c 's never sailed across it./'s never been to the Pacific.

d 's never driven one./'s never owned a motorbike.

e 's never stayed for more than six months./'s never lived in Italy.

f 've never played an instrument. /'ve never heard this group before.

6 Students' own answers.

(58) I can ... Talk about experiences and events 'before now'

1 b I've never been on a train.

c She's always loved ice cream.

d We've been to the zoo many times.

e I've never been to Kenya.

2 b She's read all the Harry Potter books.

c She's started her own website.

d She's designed beautiful baby clothes.

e She's made lots of money.

f She's written many magazine articles.

3 [Possible answers]

I have always worked here.

I have never flown a helicopter.

My best friends have always lived in Europe.

My best friends have been on a ship.

My father has been to America.

My father has never seen a kangaroo.

My teacher has seen a UFO.

My teacher has worked in Asia.

(59) I can ... Talk about work I have finished

1 b I've cleaned the bathroom.

c I've washed the clothes.

d I've bought some fresh vegetables.

e I've made the supper.

f I've phoned Kolya.

g I've told him the news.

h I've paid the electricity bill.

i I've mended the hole in the wall.

2 b Tom's opened the window.

c Brian's made the cupboard.

d Molly's cut the grass.

e Jack's mended the tap.

f Eva's painted a picture.

(60) I can ... Talk about past actions that have a result now

1 b I've broken my arm.

c Our teacher has lost her laptop.

d A bear has stolen our honey.

e They've arrived.

f You've done it again!

2 b The bus has left.

c Jen's cut her finger.

d The plane's landed.

e Mark's bought a new mobile phone.

f It's stopped raining.

(61) I can ... Say that something happened only a short time before now

1 b She's just won the race.

c She's just finished her lunch.

d He's just fallen down the ladder.

e They've just scored a goal.

f They've just broken a window.

2 b Grace has just tidied her room.

c Josh has just turned on the music.

d The baby has just fallen asleep.

e Our computer has just crashed.

f The guests have just arrived.

3 Students' own answers.

(62) I can ... Choose gone or been

1 b been **c** gone **d** gone **e** been **f** been

g been **h** gone **i** been **j** gone

2 b been **c** gone **d** been **e** gone **f** been

g gone **h** been

(63) I can ... Say that something has not happened

1 b 4 **c** 6 **d** 3 **e** 1 **f** 5

2 b I don't know. I haven't opened it yet.

c I don't know. I haven't tried it yet.

d I don't know. I haven't told him yet.

e I don't know. I haven't been to it yet.

f I don't know. I haven't met them yet.

g I don't know. I haven't done it yet.

h I don't know. I haven't rung it yet.

3 b yet **c** yet **d** just **e** yet **f** just **g** yet **h** Just

(64) I can ... Talk about actions that happened before I expected

1 b She's already been to the shops.

c The race has already started.

d I've already paid for the tickets.

e Has it already started to snow?

2 c 's already landed.

d 've already told her.

e 's already started.

f 've already seen it.

3 a 've already been to it. / been there. / visited it.

b 've already eaten it.

c 've already read it.

(65) I can ... Talk about how long things lasted

1 b since **c** for **d** since **e** since **f** for **g** since

h for **i** since **j** for

2 Students' own answers.

3 b 11.00 p.m. **c** 10.00 a.m. **d** a year **e** two nights **f** Thursday

(66) I can ... Choose whether to use Past Simple or Present Perfect

1 b lived **c** 've just found **d** Have you ever tried **e** worked

f has resigned **g** went **h** Did you have

2 b 's worked **c** worked **d** 's been **e** was

3 b did you go there?

c ever done that?

d did you go to Germany/Berlin?

e did he buy?

f has he gone?

4 Students' own answers.

(67) I can ... Talk about what people were doing at a time in the past

1 b was raining **c** was crying **d** was barking

e was ... studying **f** weren't looking

g was texting **h** was laughing

2 b I was watching **c** were you watching

d were you sitting **e** you were driving

f you were looking **g** I was having

(68) I can ... Talk about what people were doing when something else happened

1 b I was walking to work.

c I was thinking about Harry.

d I was waiting for a bus / I was standing at a bus stop.

e I was reading.

f I was swimming in the sea.

2 [possible answers]

b Sue was walking in town when she fell over.

c My friends were watching TV when I rang the bell.

d Dad was checking his email when he fell asleep.

Answer key

(69) I can ... Use verb lists

1 **b** present participle, Column 1(b)
    c Past Simple, Column 2
    d infinitive, Column 1
    e present participle, Column 1(b)
    f infinitive, Column 1

2 **b** caught, put, read **c** put **d** read **e** swim

3 **c** buy **d** cost **e** cut **f** drank **g** fallen
    h feel **i** forgotten **j** give **k** hidden **l** rode
    m run **n** spoke **o** spoken **p** threw **q** thrown
    r wear **s** worn **t** wrote **u** written

(70) I can ... Tell people about my plans

1 **b** 1, 5 **c** 4, 9 **d** 2, 6 **e** 8, 10

2 **b** I'm going to go to bed.
    c I'm going to get up.
    d I'm going to check Facebook.
    e I'm going to rescue the cat.
    f I'm going to finish the washing up.

(71) I can ... Ask and answer about what's going to happen

1 **b** What are you going to do about it?
    c Are you going to be at home at 8?
    d Are you going to go to work today?
    e What are you going to be when you grow up?
    f Are you really going to wear that?

2 **b** Are you going to see a film?
    c Which film are you going to see?
    d Is Rick going to go too?
    e Where are you going to eat after the film?
    f Are the children going to stay at home?
    g Who is going to look after them?

(72) I can ... Predict what is going to happen (because I have evidence)

1 **b** 's going to fall **c** 's going to burn
    d 's going to break down **e** 's going to cry

2 **b** The tree's going to fall. **c** They're going to crash.
    d It's going to snow. **e** He's going to score (a goal).
    f He's going to go swimming.

3 **c** Sales are going to fall. **d** Factory 72 is going to close.
    e The company's going to make an important new product.
    f The company's going to win an award/a 'Best new product' award.
    g Our/The company's HQ is going to move to Africa.
    h The company's going to give $1 billion to charity.
    i The company's going to employ another 350 people.

4 [possible answers]
    a He's going to rob the house./ He's going to break the window./ He's going to steal their money.
    b She's going to dance in the school play. / She's going to fall. / She's going to be a star. / She's going to be a ballet dancer.

5 [possible answers]
    b 'm going to miss the train. **c** 're going to get married.
    d are going to fall. **e** 'm going to be sick.
    f 're going to take the PET exam.

(73) I can ... Say who things happened to

1 **b** me **c** them **d** her **e** us **f** you

2 **c** her **d** him **e** They **f** them **g** him **h** He
    i them **j** them **k** We **l** us

3 A **b** 3 **c** 1
    B **a** 3 **b** 2 **c** 1
    C **a** 3 **b** 1 **c** 2
    D **a** 2 **b** 1 **c** 3

4 **b** to **c** with **d** to **e** about **f** to **g** with
    h for **i** at **j** for

(74) I can ... Say who things belong to

1 **b** your **c** her **d** hers **e** my **f** mine **g** theirs **h** ours
    i our

2 Students' own answers.

3 **b** brothers **c** brothers' **d** brother's **e** parents
    f children's **g** boys **h** boys' **i** boy's

4 **c** Who's **d** Whose **e** Who's **f** Who's
    g whose **h** who's **i** Whose **j** Who's

(75) I can ... Make plurals

1 **c** three women **d** two knives **e** five people
    f three watches **g** four feet **h** eight sheep
    i two shelves **j** nine leaves **k** three buses

2 **b** How many ~~child~~ **children** do you have?
    c Please put these ~~knife~~ **knives** on the table.
    d We went to ~~some~~ **a** wonderful party last week! /We went to some wonderful ~~party~~ **parties** last week!
    e There are lots of beautiful ~~tree~~ **trees** in this forest.
    f Where ~~are~~ **is** the English-Chinese dictionary? /Where are the English-Chinese ~~dictionary~~ **dictionaries**?
    g William bought twelve ~~egg~~ **eggs** and six ~~sausage~~ **sausages**.
    h I have three credit ~~card~~ **cards** and I spend too much money!
    i How many English ~~teacher~~ **teachers** work in your school?
    j The washing machine ~~are~~ **is** in the basement. /The washing ~~machine~~ **machines** are in the basement.
    k I always buy all my train ~~ticket~~ **tickets** online.
    l Jane met lots of interesting ~~person~~ **people** at the meeting.
    m This computer game is so hard! I've only got two ~~life~~ **lives** left!

(76) I can ... Use *a* and *an*

1 **c** a **d** a **e** an **f** an **g** an **h** a **i** a **j** a **k** a **l** an

2 **b** It's an egg. **c** It's an apple. **d** It's an iron.
    e It's a scarf. **f** It's a bottle. **g** It's a handbag.

3 **b** He's a doctor. **c** She's a pilot. **d** He's an artist.
    e She's an athlete.

4 **b** a **c** a **d** an **e** an, an **f** a, an, a **g** an
    h a, an **i** a

(77) I can ... Decide whether to use *a*, *an* or *the*

1 **b** a, a **c** a, the **d** an, the **e** a, a, the, a **f** a, a **g** a, a
    h an, the **i** a, the **j** a, the, the **k** a, The, The, the, a
    l an, the **m** The, a **n** the **o** a, a, A, the **p** a, a, A, a

2 **c** the **d** the **e** an **f** the **g** the **h** the **i** a **j** the **k** the
    l a **m** the **n** a **o** a **p** a **q** the **r** a **s** The **t** the **u** the
    v the **w** a **x** a **y** a **z** the

(78) I can ... Decide when *the* isn't needed

1 **b** the picture **c** New York **d** tennis
    e the Princess **f** the town centre
    g Peter and Sara **h** the new car **i** home
    j the Moon **k** the song **l** Geography

2 **c** Ø, Ø **d** the **e** Ø **f** Ø **g** Ø **h** the, the **i** Ø
    j the **k** Ø, Ø **l** Ø **m** the

(79) I can ... Say why things happened

1 **b** 4 **c** 7 **d** 1 **e** 6 **f** 3 **g** 5

2 **c** buy some concert tickets
    d he could tell her about the prize
    e open the program
    f she could do more exercise

3 **b** to see / so that they can see pandas
    c to study / so that he could study
    d to save / so that they can save lives

(80) I can ... Tell people what to do

1 **b** Go away! **c** Don't forget! **d** Be quiet! **e** Hurry up!
    f Wait here. **g** Don't lose your temper! **h** Tell me!
    i Say cheese! **j** Slow down! **k** Come back! **l** Have fun!

2 c Close your book. **d** Click here. **e** Stop!
f Don't take photos. **g** Be quiet. **h** Don't feed the animals.
i Don't disturb. **j** Look at that. / Look!

3 b Let's go to the cinema. **c** Let's have a drink.
d Let's play chess. / Let's have a game of chess.
e Let's play tennis. / Let's have a game of tennis.
f Let's go to Paris.

4 b Let's start! **c** Let's ask! **d** Let's go back!
e Let's try again! **f** Let's walk! **g** Let's wait!
h Let's get some food!

(81) I can ... Use countable and mass nouns

1 c (C) pens **d** (U) **e** (C/U) teas **f** (C) teeth
g (C) people **h** (U) **i** (U) **j** (C/U) orange juices
k (U) **l** (C) £10 notes **m** (U) **n** (U)
o (C) newspapers **p** (C/U) papers
q (C) coats **r** (C) fathers

2 c some **d** a **e** some **f** some **g** a **h** some

3 c Have you done your ~~homeworks~~ **homework**?
d She gave Betty some very important ~~advices~~ **advice**.
e I don't like the ~~weathers~~ **weather** today.
f I heard ~~a~~ **some** really interesting news.
g Have you got any ~~informations~~ **information** about train times to London?
h We had ~~funs~~ **fun** at the carnival.
i He bought some ~~flours~~ **flour** at the supermarket.
j You have beautiful ~~hairs~~ **hair**.

4 b newspapers, news **c** cars, traffic
d exercises, homework **e** chairs, furniture
f coins, money **g** clouds, weather

(82) I can ... Ask people what they would like (food, drink, etc.)

1 b a **c** some **d** some **e** a **f** some **g** a
h some **i** a **j** some **k** some **l** a **m** some

(83) I can ... Talk about quantities of uncountable things

1 b 3,I, M **c** 15, K **d** 4, L **e** 2, F, G, J
f 8, H, I, M, N **g** 11, C **h** 1, O **i** 14, E, I **j** 7, A **k** 12,
H **l** 13, D **m** 10, C, F, M, N **n** 5, F, G, J, O **o** 9, A, B, K

2 b bar **c** bag **d** bottle **e** tank **f** packet **g** jar
h packet **i** litre / bottle **j** kilo / slice

(84) I can ... Ask if people have things

1 b any **c** any **d** some **e** any **f** some
g any **h** some **i** some **j** any

2 c catch any **d** ironed some **e** pick some
f cooked some **g** remember any **h** want any

3 b some information True **c** Some sharks True
d any islands False **e** any exercises False
f Some skyscrapers False

(85) I can ... Ask and answer about quantities

1 b How much, How many **c** How many, How much
d How much, How many **e** How much, How many
f How many, How much **g** How much, How many
h How many, How much **i** How much, How many
j How many, How much **k** How many, How much
l How many, How much **m** How much, How many

2 b watch much TV. **c** give us much information.
d eat much dessert. **e** have much money in her purse.
f much milk in the fridge. **g** have much time to practise.

3 c ✗ much is not possible **d** ✗ much is not possible
e ✓ much is possible **f** ✓ much is possible
g ✗ much is not possible **h** ✓ much is possible

4 [Possible answers]
Bears don't eat many sandwiches.
How many sandwiches did Polly make?
How much honey did the bears eat?

Polly didn't eat much honey.
Polly didn't see many bears.
Polly doesn't eat a lot of sandwiches.
Polly made lots of honey sandwiches.
The bears ate lots of honey.

(86) I can ... Say how we do things

1 c happily **d** correct **e** fast **f** violent **g** well
h honest **i** formally **j** gently **k** fluent

2 c well **d** good **e** perfectly **f** perfect **g** fluently
h strong **i** angrily **j** quietly

3 c carefully **d** correctly **e** wrongly **f** gently **g** well

4 Students' own answers.

(87) I can ... Say what was in a place in the past

1 b There were **c** There was **d** There was
e There were **f** There was **g** There was
h There were

2 b Were there **c** Was there **d** Were there
e Was there **f** Was there **g** Were there

(88) I can... Say what I have just decided to do

1 b 5 **c** 7 **d** 2 **e** 6 **f** 3 **g** 1

2 b I'll lend you some. **c** I'll give her some food.
d I'll get it. **e** I'll Google it. **f** I'll change the batteries.

3 Students' own answers.

(89) I can ... Say what I think will happen

1 b an offer to help **c** a warning or threat
d asking for help **e** a promise **f** an offer to help

2 b will, won't **c** won't, will **d** 'll, won't
e will, won't **f** Will, won't **g** won't, 'll **h** will, won't

3 b Will you live in a foreign country? Yes, I will. / Yes, I might. / No, I won't. / No, I might not.
c Will you study another language? Yes, I will. / Yes, I might. / No, I won't. / No, I might not.
d Will you celebrate your next birthday? Yes, I will. / Yes, I might. / No, I won't. / No, I might not.
e Will you become very rich? Yes, I will. / Yes, I might. / No, I won't. / No, I might not.

4 b Shall I tidy it? **c** Shall I tell her? **d** Shall I change it?
e Shall I lend him some?

5 Students' own answers.

(90) I can ... Talk about things I have, make or do

1 c do **d** have **e** make **f** do **g** make **h** have
i make **j** make **k** do **l** have **m** make

2 b do **c** has **d** made **e** making **f** make
g having **h** make

3 b do **c** make **d** have **e** do **f** make
g have **h** do **i** has

4 b made, penicillin **c** made, eggs **d** had, sleep
e made, Moon **f** had, poem

(91) I can ... Choose the right auxiliary verb

1 c is **d** Does **e** Is **f** is **g** Has **h** does **i** has **j** is

2 c has **d** is **e** is **f** has **g** has

3 b doesn't **c** isn't **d** hasn't **e** haven't **f** aren't
g don't **h** aren't

4 b Did **c** Did **d** Were **e** Did **f** Was **g** Did

5 a one **b** two **c** more than one **d** one car
e now **f** in the past **g** a main verb
h an auxiliary verb

6 2 Sentence c – The cars arrived.
3 Sentence e – We're there.
4 Sentence a – My hand's cold.
5 Sentence f – We were there.
6 Sentence g – We have one.

Answer key

92 **I can ... Talk about things I like and dislike doing**

1 **b** to watch **c** to visit / visiting **d** going
e to have / having **f** to see **g** to listen / listening

2 **b** to buy **c** going **d** eating **e** hearing **f** to stay / staying

93 **I can ... Talk about things I was able to do in the past**

1 **b** I couldn't sleep last night.
c I couldn't find my glasses.
d I couldn't understand the announcements.
e I couldn't start the car.
f I couldn't answer any of the questions.

2 Students' own answers.

94 **I can ... Say that something is really important to do**

1 **b** You must lock the door.
c You must wear a seat belt.
d You must wash your hands.
e You must be 130 cms tall.
f You must take off your helmet.
g You must show your passport.
h You must drive very slowly.

2 **b** I must call Harry.
c I must finish my homework.
d I must eat (something).
e I must update my Facebook page.

3 **b** You mustn't wake up the baby.
c You mustn't press that button.
d You mustn't run near the swimming pool.
e You mustn't disturb your father.
f You mustn't worry.
g You mustn't tell her.

95 **I can ... Listen to other people's advice**

1 **b** 1 **c** 4 **d** 8 **e** 2 **f** 5 **g** 6 **h** 7

2 [Possible answers]
a You shouldn't drink so much coffee.
You should drink some water.
You should sleep more. / You should go to bed early.
You should turn off the TV.
b You should do some work.
You should read your chemistry books.
You shouldn't go out every night.
c You shouldn't drive very fast. / You should drive carefully /
slow down.
You shouldn't eat while you are driving.
You should put on your seat belt.
You should lock your car. / You should get insurance.

3 **b** Should I call her?
c Should I leave home?
d Should I dye my hair?
e Should I remind him?
f Should I forget about it?
g Should I tell Nick?

4 [Possible answers]
b I think you should slow down / drive more slowly.
c I think you should tidy up.
d I think you should take your exam again / study hard.
e I think you should go to bed.
f I think you should have a rest.

96 **I can ... Say how people and things are different**

1 **b** sadder **c** easier **d** larger **e** prettier
f bigger **g** better **h** wiser **i** lovelier
j worse **k** wetter

2 **b** The thief's taller than the wizard.
c The thief is younger than the wizard.
d The wizard is kinder than the troll.
e The thief is stronger than the elf.
f The wizard is weaker than the thief.
g The wizard is shorter than the elf.
h The elf is healthier than the troll.
i The elf is cleverer than the thief.

3 **b** thinner **c** weaker **d** slower **e** quieter
f lighter **g** worse

4 Students' own answers.

5 **b** The Great Pyramid at Giza is older than the Taj Mahal.
c Taipei 101 is taller than The Shard in London.
d The Sahara desert is hotter than the Karakum desert.
e The Sahara desert is bigger than the Karakum desert.
f The Karakum desert is rainier than the Sahara desert.

97 **I can ... Compare books, films and other things**

1 **c** more successful **d** lighter **e** more modern
f more delicious **g** simpler **h** more comfortable
i more popular **j** windier **k** more relaxed **l** hotter
m more confident

2 **b** more expensive **c** less comfortable **d** more careful
e less frequent **f** more personal **g** more valuable

3 **b** less comfortable than the sofa.
c more difficult than Question 7.
d less modern than the Cottonly Centre.
e less likely to pass the exam than Sue.
f less active than Penny.
g more popular than Rainy Fields.
h less detailed than the maps in the red book.

4 **b** My robot is slower than yours.
c My robot is less efficient than yours.
d My robot is more expensive than yours.
e My robot is heavier than yours.
f My robot is more annoying than yours.
g My robot is more likely to go wrong than yours.

98 **I can ... Say which things are the 'most'**

1 **c** the loudest **d** the most enjoyable **e** the tidiest
f the most delicious **g** the loveliest **h** the widest
i the most beautiful

2 **b** The Pushkin **c** The Chaika **d** The Chaika
e The Chaika **f** The Metropole **g** The Pushkin

3 Students' own answers.

4 **b** the most dangerous **c** the longest **d** the oldest
e the largest **f** the most valuable

99 **I can ... Tell a joke**

1 **b** 9 **c** 7 **d** 2 **e** 4 **f** 8 **g** 5 **h** 1 **i** 6

2 **b** sits **c** asks **d** replies **e** opens **f** bites
g screams **h** said **i** doesn't

3 Students' own answers.